THE HEART OF CHRIST

From the original title page of this work

THE

HEART

OF

CHRIST In Heaven

Towards

Sinners on Earth.

OR,

A TREATISE

DEMONSTRATING

The gracious Disposition and tender
Affection of *Christ* in his Humane Nature now in
Glory, unto his Members under all sorts of
Infirmities, either of *Sin* or *Misery*

THE
HEART OF CHRIST

Thomas Goodwin

THE BANNER OF TRUTH TRUST

THE BANNER OF TRUTH TRUST
3 Murrayfield Road, Edinburgh EH12 6EL, UK
P.O. Box 621, Carlisle, PA 17013, USA

*

First published as *The Heart of Christ in Heaven
Towards Sinners on Earth* 1651
Reprinted from the 1862 Nichol edition of
The Works of Thomas Goodwin, D.D., Volume 4
This edition © The Banner of Truth Trust, 2011

ISBN: 978 1 84871 146 4

*

Typeset in 11/15 pt Sabon Oldstyle at
The Banner of Truth Trust, Edinburgh.

Printed in the USA by
Versa Press, Inc.,
East Peoria, IL

CONTENTS

Editorial Note:

Footnotes from the Nichol Edition of Goodwin's *Works* are attributed to 'Ed.' as they appear in the 1862 edition. The present publisher has added explanations of a few words which may not be familiar to current readers—these are attributed to 'P.' A small number of spellings has been modernised. Latin and Greek renderings have been retained, as the English meaning is usually clear from the text, or is explained in a 'P' footnote.

FOREWORD

HOW can Thomas Goodwin be so forgotten? Once ranked as a theologian alongside Augustine and Athanasius, even hailed as 'the greatest pulpit exegete of Paul that has ever lived', he should be a household name.[1] His writings, while not easy, always pay back the reader, for in Goodwin a simply awesome theological intellect was wielded by the tender heart of a pastor.

As it is, Goodwin needs a little re-introduction. He was born in 1600 in the small village of Rollesby in Norfolk. His parents were God-fearing, and at that time the Norfolk Broads were well-soaked in Puritanism, so unsurprisingly he grew up somewhat religious. That all wore off, though, when he went up to Cambridge as a student. There he divided his time between 'making merry' and setting out to become a celebrity preacher. He wanted, he later said, to be known as one of 'the great wits' of the pulpit, for his 'master-lust' was the love of applause.

[1] G. F. Barbour, *The Life of Alexander Whyte* (London, 1925), p. 82; P. T. Forsyth, *The Principle of Authority* (London: Independent Press, 1913), p. 273.

Then in 1620—having just been appointed a fellow of Katharine Hall—he heard a funeral sermon that actually moved him, making him deeply concerned for his spiritual state. It started seven grim years of moody introspection as he grubbed around inside himself for signs of grace. Only when he was told to look outwards—not to trust to anything in himself, but to rest on Christ alone—only then was he free. 'I am come to this pass now', he said, 'that signs will do me no good alone; I have trusted too much to habitual grace for assurance of justification; I tell you Christ is worth all.'[1]

Soon afterwards he took over from Richard Sibbes' preaching at Holy Trinity Church. It was an appropriate transition, for while in his navel-gazing days his preaching had been mostly about battering consciences, his appreciation of Christ's free grace now made him a Christ-centred preacher like Sibbes. Sibbes once told him 'Young man, if ever you would do good, you must preach the gospel and the free grace of God in Christ Jesus'—and that is just what Goodwin now did. And, like Sibbes, he became an affable preacher. He wouldn't use his intellectual abilities to patronise his listeners, but to help them. Still today, reading his sermons, it is as if he takes you by the shoulder and walks with you like a brother.

[1] *The Works of Thomas Goodwin* (Edinburgh: James Nichol, 1861-1866), 2.lxx.

All the while, Archbishop Laud was pressing clergy towards his own 'high church' practices. By 1634, Goodwin had had enough: he resigned his post and left Cambridge to become a Separatist preacher. By the end of the decade he was with other Nonconformist exiles in Holland. Then, in 1641, Parliament invited all such Nonconformists to return, and soon Goodwin was leading the 'dissenting brethren' at the Westminster Assembly. 'Dissenting', 'Separatist': it would be easy to see Goodwin as prickly and quarrelsome. In actual fact, though, while he was definite in his views on the church, he was quite extraordinarily charitable to those he disagreed with, and managed to command widespread respect across the theological spectrum of the church. Almost uniquely, in an age of constant and often bitter debate, nobody seems to have spoken ill of Goodwin.

If there was a contemporary Goodwin overlapped with more than any other, it was John Owen. In the Puritan heyday of the 1650s, when Owen was Vice-Chancellor of Oxford University, Goodwin was President of Magdalen College. For years they shared a Sunday afternoon pulpit, both were chaplains to Cromwell, together they would co-author the *Savoy Declaration*. And both had their own sartorial whimsies: Owen was known for his dandy day-wear, his snake-bands and fancy boots; Goodwin, it was giggled, had such a fondness for nightcaps that he is said to have worn whole collections on his head at once.

First and foremost, Goodwin was a pastor at heart. Students at Magdalen College soon found that, should they bump into Goodwin or his nightcaps, they could expect to be asked when they were converted or how they stood with the Lord. And when Charles II returned in 1660 and Goodwin was deprived of his post, it was to pastor a church in London that he went.

The last twenty years of his life he spent pastoring, writing treatises, and studying in London (the study sadly interrupted in 1666 when the Great Fire burned more than half of his voluminous library). Then, at eighty years of age, he was gripped by a fatal fever. With his dying words he captured what had always been his chief concerns: 'I am going', he said,

> to the three Persons, with whom I have had communion . . . My bow abides in strength. Is Christ divided? No, I have the whole of his righteousness; I am found in him, not having my own righteousness, which is of the law, but the righteousness which is of God, which is by faith of Jesus Christ, who loved me, and gave himself for me. Christ cannot love me better than he doth. I think I cannot love Christ better than I do; I am swallowed up in God . . . Now I shall be ever with the Lord.[1]

[1] *Works*, 2.lxxiv–lxxv.

The Heart of Christ in Heaven towards Sinners on Earth was, almost immediately, Goodwin's most popular work. It is also exemplary of his overall Christ-centredness and his mix of theological rigour and pastoral concern. Published in 1651 alongside *Christ Set Forth*, the two were written for reasons dear to Goodwin: that is, he felt that many Christians (like himself once) 'have been too much carried away with the rudiments of Christ in their own hearts, and not after Christ himself'. Indeed, he wrote, 'the minds of many are so wholly taken up with their own hearts, that (as the Psalmist says of God) Christ "is scarce in all their thoughts".'[1] Goodwin wanted us 'first to look wholly out of our selves unto Christ', and believed that the reason we don't is, quite simply, because of the 'barrenness' of our knowledge of him.[2] Thus Goodwin would set forth Christ to draw our gaze to him.

Of the two pieces, *Christ Set Forth* and *The Heart of Christ in Heaven*, the latter was the cream, he believed, for through it he would present to the church the heart of her great Husband, thus wooing her afresh. His specific aim in this essay is to show through Scripture that in all his heavenly majesty, Christ is not now aloof from believers and unconcerned, but has the strongest affections for them. And knowing this, he said, may

[1] *Works*, 4.3.
[2] *Works*, 4.4.

hearten and encourage believers to come more boldly unto the throne of grace, unto such a Saviour and High Priest, when they shall know how sweetly and tenderly his heart, though he is now in his glory, is inclined towards them.[1]

Goodwin starts with Christ on earth and the beautiful assurances he gave his disciples. In John 13, for example, knowing that he was shortly to return to his Father, Jesus washed his disciples' feet as a token of how he would always be towards them; he told them of how he would go like a loving bridegroom to prepare a place for his bride; after the resurrection, the first thing he calls them is 'my brothers'; and the last thing they see as he ascends to heaven is his hands raised in blessing.

It is as if he had said, The truth is, I cannot live without you, I shall never be quiet till I have you where I am, that so we may never part again; that is the reason of it. Heaven shall not hold me, nor my Father's company, if I have not you with me, my heart is so set upon you; and if I have any glory, you shall have part of it . . . Poor sinners, who are full of the thoughts of their own sins, know not how they shall be able at the latter day to look Christ in the face when they shall first meet with him. But they may relieve their spirits against their care and fear, by Christ's carriage now towards his disciples, who had so sinned against him. Be not afraid,

---

[1] *Works*, 4.95; (see p. 2 below).

'your sins will he remember no more' . . . And doth he talk thus lovingly of us? Whose heart would not this overcome?[1]

It is moving stuff, and it is strong stuff. In fact, Goodwin presents the kindness and compassion of Christ so strikingly that, when reading him, I find myself continually asking 'Is Goodwin serious? Can this really be true?' He argues, for example, that in Christ's resurrection appearances, because he had dealt with the sin of his disciples on the cross, 'No sin of theirs troubled him but their unbelief.'[2] And yet Goodwin is so carefully scriptural that one is forced to conclude that Christ really is more tender and loving than we would otherwise dare to imagine.

Then Goodwin takes us to the heart of his argument: his exposition of Hebrews 4:15, which

doth, as it were, take our hands, and lay them upon Christ's breast, and let us feel how his heart beats and his bowels yearn towards us, even now he is in glory—the very scope of these words being manifestly to encourage believers against all that may discourage them, from the consideration of Christ's heart towards them now in heaven.[3]

---

[1] *Works*, 4.100, 105 (pp. 16, 31 below).
[2] *Works*, 4.106 (p. 32 below).
[3] *Works*, 4.111 (p. 48 below).

Goodwin shows that in all his glorious holiness in heaven, Christ is not sour towards his people; if anything, his capacious heart beats *more* strongly than ever with tender love for them. And in particular, two things stir his compassion: our afflictions and—almost unbelievably—our sins.

Having experienced on earth the utmost load of pain, rejection and sorrow, 'in all points tempted like as we are', Christ in heaven empathises with our sufferings more fully than the most loving friend. And more: he has compassion on those who are 'out of the way' (that is, sinning; *Heb.* 5:2). Indeed, says Goodwin,

> your very sins move him to pity more than to anger . . . yea, his pity is increased the more towards you, even as the heart of a father is to a child that hath some loathsome disease . . . his hatred shall all fall, and that only upon the sin, to free you of it by its ruin and destruction, but his bowels shall be the more drawn out to you; and this as much when you lie under sin as under any other affliction. Therefore fear not, 'What shall separate us from Christ's love?'[1]

The focus is upon Christ, but Goodwin was ardently Trinitarian and could not abide the thought of his readers imagining a compassionate Christ appeasing a heartless Father. No, he said, 'Christ adds not one

---

[1] *Works*, 4.149 (p. 156 below).

drop of love to God's heart.'[1] All Christ's tenderness comes in fact from the Spirit, who stirs him with the very love of the Father. The heart of Christ in heaven is the express image of the heart of his Father.

How we need Goodwin and his message today! If we are to be drawn from jaded, anxious thoughts of God and a love of sin, we need such a knowledge of Christ. If preachers today could change like Goodwin to preach like Goodwin, who knows what might happen? Surely many more would then say as he said 'Christ cannot love me better than he doth. I think I cannot love Christ better than I do'.[2]

MICHAEL REEVES
Oxford
August 2011

---

[1] *Works*, 4.86.
[2] *Works*, 2.lxxiv-lxxv.

PART 1

OUTWARD DEMONSTRATIONS OF THE TENDERNESS OF CHRIST'S HEART TOWARDS SINNERS

HAVING set forth our Lord and Saviour Jesus Christ[1] in all those great and most solemn actions of his—his obedience unto death, his resurrection, ascension into heaven, his sitting at God's right hand, and intercession for us, which of all the other hath been more largely insisted on—I shall now annex (as next in order, and homogeneal thereunto) this discourse that follows, which lays open *the heart* of Christ, as now he is in

[1] The reference is to Goodwin's treatise on Romans 8:34, *Christ Set Forth*, which preceded *The Heart of Christ in Heaven Towards Sinners on Earth* in a single volume first published in 1651.

heaven, sitting at God's right hand and interceding for us; how it is affected and graciously disposed towards sinners on earth that do come to him; how willing to receive them; how ready to entertain them; how tender to pity them in all their infirmities, both sins and miseries. The scope and use whereof will be this, to hearten and encourage believers to come more boldly unto the throne of grace, unto such a Saviour and High Priest, when they shall know how sweetly and tenderly his heart, though he is now in his glory, is inclined towards them; and so to remove that great stone of stumbling which we meet with (and yet lieth unseen) in the thoughts of men in the way to faith, that Christ being now absent, and withal exalted so high and infinite a distance of glory, as to 'sit at God's right hand', *etc.*, they therefore cannot tell how to come to treat with him about their salvation so freely, and with that hopefulness to obtain, as those poor sinners did, who were here on earth with him. Had our lot been, think they, but to have conversed with him in the days of his flesh, as Mary, and Peter, and his other disciples did here below, we could have thought to have been bold with him, and to have had anything at his hands. For they beheld him afore them a man like unto themselves, and he was full of meekness and gentleness, he being then himself made sin, and sensible of all sorts of miseries; but now he is gone into a far country, and hath put on glory and immortality, and how his heart may be altered thereby we know not. The drift of this discourse is therefore to ascertain poor souls, that his heart, in respect of pity and compassion, remains the same it was on earth; that he intercedes there with the same heart he did here below; and that he is as meek, as gentle, as easy to be entreated, as tender in his affections;[1] so that they may deal with him as fairly about the great matter of their salvation, and as hopefully, and upon as easy terms to obtain it of him, as they might if they had been on earth with him, and with him in all their needs—than which nothing can be more for the comfort and encouragement of those who have given over all other lives but that of faith, and whose souls pursue after strong and entire communion with their Saviour Christ.

Now the demonstrations that may help our faith in this I reduce to two heads: the first more extrinsical and outward; the second more intrinsical and

---

[1] The original has 'bowels', derived from the ancient idea of the bowels or kidneys being the seat of the affections, much as the 'heart' is seen today. Compare, for example, the AV rendering of Song of Solomon 5:4 with modern translations. A similar change has been made throughout, where appropriate.—P.

inward: the one showing the ὅτι of it, *that it is so;* the other the διότι, the *reasons* and *grounds* why it must be so.

I. First, for those *extrinsical demonstrations* (as I call them), they are taken from several passages and carriages of his, in all those several conditions of his; namely, at his last farewell afore his death, his resurrection, ascension, and how he is sitting at God's right hand. I shall lead you through all the same heads which I have gone over in the former treatise (though to another purpose), and take such observations from his speeches and carriages, in all those states he went through, as shall tend directly to persuade our hearts of the point in hand, namely this, that now he is heaven, his heart remains as graciously inclined to sinners that come to him, as ever on earth. And for a ground or introduction to these first sort of demonstrations, I shall take this Scripture that follows; as for those other, another Scripture, as proper to that part of this discourse.

When Jesus knew that his hour was come, that he should depart out of this world unto the Father, having loved his own, he loved them to the end; [or for ever]—(John 13:1).

Demonstrations from Christ's last farewell to his disciples

I. It was long before that Christ did break his mind to his disciples that he was to leave them, and to go away to heaven from them, for, he says, he had forborne 'to tell it them from the beginning' (*John* 16:4). But when he begins to acquaint them with it, he then at once leaves them an abundance of his heart, and that not only how it stood towards them, and what it was at the present, but what it would be when he should be in his glory. Let us, to this end, but briefly peruse his last carriage, and his sermon at his last supper which he did eat with them, as it is on purpose penned and recorded by the evangelist John; and we shall find this to be the drift of those long discourses of Christ's, from the 13th to the 18th chapter. I will not make a comment on them, but only briefly take up such short observations as do more specially hold forth this thing in hand.

1. These words which I have prefixed as the text, are the preface unto all that his discourse that follows (namely, unto that washing of his disciples' feet, and his succeeding sermon), which accordingly do show the argument and sum of all. The preface is this: 'Before the feast of the Passover, when Jesus

knew that his hour was come, that he should depart out of this world unto the Father, having loved his own which were in the world, he loved them unto the end. And supper being ended, Jesus knowing that the Father had given all things into his hands, and that he was come from God, and went to God, he then washed his disciples' feet.'

Now this preface was prefixed by the evangelist, on purpose to set open a window into Christ's heart, to show what it was then at his departure, and so withal to give a light into, and put a gloss and interpretation upon all that follows. The scope whereof is to show what his affections would be to them in heaven: he tells us what Christ's thoughts were then, and what was his heart amidst those thoughts, both which occasioned all that succeeds.

(1.) He premiseth what was in Christ's thoughts and his meditation. He began deeply to consider, both that he was to depart out of this world, 'Jesus knew', *etc.*, says the text (that is, was then thinking of it), 'that he should depart unto the Father', and how that then he should shortly be installed into that glory which was due unto him; so it follows, verse 3, 'Jesus knowing' (that is, was then actually taking into his mind) 'that the Father had given all things into his hands', that is, that all power in heaven and earth was his, so soon as he should set footing in heaven; then in the midst of these thoughts he tells us, he went and washed his disciples' feet, after he had first considered whither he was to go, and there what he was to be.

(2.) But, secondly, what was Christ's heart most upon, in the midst of all these elevated meditations? Not upon his own glory so much, though it is told us that he considered that, thereby the more to set out his love unto us, but upon these thoughts his heart ran out in love towards, and was set upon, 'his own': 'having loved his own', says the first verse, τους ἰδιους, his own, a word denoting the greatest nearness, dearness, and intimateness founded upon propriety.[1] The elect are Christ's own, a piece of himself, not τα ἰδια, as goods, 'he came unto his own, and his own received him not' (*John* 1:11); τα ἰδια, the word shows that he reckons them his own, but as goods, not as persons, but he calls these here τους ἰδιους, his own by a nearer propriety, that is, his own children, his own member, his own wife, his own flesh; and he considers, that though he was to go out of the world, yet they were to be in the world, and therefore it is on purpose added, 'which were in the world,' that is, to remain, in this world. He had others

---

[1] That is, 'property', or 'ownership'. —Ed.

of his own who were in that world unto which he was going, even 'the spirits of just men made perfect', whom as yet he had never seen. One would think, that when he was meditating upon his going out of this world, his heart should be all upon Abraham, his Isaacs, and his Jacobs, whom he was going to; no, he takes more care for his own, who were to remain here in this world, a world wherein there is much evil (as himself says, *John* 17:15), both of sin and misery, and with which themselves, whilst in it, could not but be defiled and vexed. This is it which draws out his affections towards them, even at that time when his heart was full of the thoughts of his own glory: 'having loved his own, he loved them unto the end'. Which is spoken to show the constancy of his love, and what it would be when Christ should be in his glory. 'To the end', that is, to the perfection of it, εἰς τελείωσιν, says Chrysostom; having begun to love them, he will perfect and consummate his love to them. And 'to the end', that is, for ever. So in the Greek, εἰς τέλος is sometimes used, and so by the evangelist the phrase is here used in a suitableness to the Scripture phrase, 'He will not always chide, nor reserve anger *for ever*' (*Psa.* 103:9), so we translate it; but in the original, 'He reserves not anger *unto the end.*' So that the scope of this speech is to show how

8

Christ's heart and love would be towards them even *for ever,* when he should be gone unto his Father, as, well as it was to show how it had been here on earth, they being his own; and he having loved them, he alters, he changes not, and therefore will love them for ever. pray to understand and believe more fully!

(3.) And then thirdly, to testify thus much by a real testimony, what his love would be, when in heaven, to them, the evangelist shows, that when he was in the midst of all those great thoughts of his approaching glory, and of the sovereign estate which he was to be in, he then took water and a towel, and washed his disciples' feet. This to have been his scope will appear, if you observe but the coherence in the second verse, it is said, that 'Jesus knowing that the Father had given all things into his hands' then 'he riseth from supper, and lays aside his garments, and took a towel and girded himself' (verse 4), after that, 'he poured water into a bason, and began to wash his disciples' feet', *etc.* (verse 5), where it is evident that the evangelist's scope is to hold forth this unto us, that then when Christ's thoughts were full of his glory, and when he took in the consideration of it unto the utmost, even then, and upon that occasion, and in the midst of those thoughts, he washed his disciples' feet. And what was

Christ's meaning in this, but that, whereas when he should be in heaven, he could not make such outward visible demonstrations of his heart, by doing such mean services for them; therefore by doing this in the midst of such thoughts of his glory, he would show what he could be content (as it were) to do for them, when he should be in full possession of it? So great is his love unto them. There is another expression of Christ's like unto this, in Luke 12:36, 37, which confirms this to be his meaning here, and to be his very heart in heaven. At verse 36, he compares himself to a bridegroom, who is to go to heaven unto a wedding-feast; who hath servants on earth that stand all that while here below, as without, waiting for him; at which, because they wait so long, they may think much, Christ adds, 'Verily I say unto you, that when the bridegroom returns' (refreshed with wine and gladness) 'he shall gird himself, and make them sit down to meat, and will come forth and serve them.' The meaning is not as if that Christ served at the latter day, or now in heaven, those that sit down there; but only it is an abundant expression in words, as here in a real instance, to set forth the overflowing love that is in his heart, and the transcendent happiness that we shall then enjoy, even beyond what can be expected by us; he utters himself therefore by an unwonted thing not heard of, that the Lord should serve his servants, and wait on them that waited for him. And it is to show his heart to them, and what he could be contented to do for them. So that you see what his heart was before he went to heaven, even amidst the thoughts of all his glory; and you see what it is after he hath been in heaven, and greatened with all his glory, even content to wash poor sinners' feet, and to serve them that come to him and wait for him.

(4.) Now, fourthly, what was the mystery of this his washing their feet? It was, as to give them an example of mutual love and humility, so to signify his washing away their sins; thus, verses 8 and 10, himself interprets it. It is true indeed, that, now he is in heaven, he cannot come to wash the feet of their bodies, but he would signify thus much thereby, that those sinners that will come to him when in his glory, he will wash away all their sins; 'He loved his church, and gave himself for it, that he might sanctify and cleanse it with the washing of water, that he might present it to himself a glorious church, not having spot or wrinkle,' *etc.* (*Eph.* 5:25-27).

2. This specimen or declaration of his mind, we have from this his carriage, at this his last farewell. Let us next take a survey of the drift of that long

sermon which he made at that his farewell, and we shall find the main scope of it to be further to assure his disciples of what his heart would be unto them; and that will make a second demonstration.

It were too long a work to insist upon each particular. But certainly, no loving husband ever endeavoured more to satisfy the heart of his spouse during his absence, than Christ doth his disciples' hearts, and in them all believers. For take that along, once for all, that what Christ said unto them, he says unto us, as in that 17th of John that speech implies, 'I pray not for them only, but for those also that shall believe through their word.' And as what he prayed for them was for all believers also, so what he then spake unto them.

(1.) First, he lets them see what his heart would be unto them, and how mindful of them when in heaven, by that business which he professeth he went thither to perform for them; concerning which, observe first, that he lovingly acquaints them with it aforehand what it is, which argued care and tenderness, as from an husband unto a wife it doth. And withal, how plain-heartedly doth he speak, as one that would not hide anything from them! 'I tell you the truth of it' (says he), 'it is expedient, and expedient for you, that I go away' (*John* 16:7). And secondly, he tells them, it is wholly for them and their happiness, 'I go to send you a comforter', whilst you are in this world, and 'to prepare a place for you' (*John* 14:2), when you shall go out of this world. 'There are many mansions in my Father's house', and I go to take them up for you, and to keep your places for you till you come. And there again, how openly and candidly doth he speak to them! 'If it had been otherwise', says he, 'I would have told you.' You may believe me, I would not deceive you for all the glory in that place to which I am a-going. Whom would not this openness and nakedness of heart persuade? But then, thirdly, the business itself being such as is so much for us and our happiness, how much more doth that argue it. And indeed, Christ himself doth fetch from thence an argument of the continuance of his love to them. So verse 3, 'If I go to prepare a place for you, if that be my errand, then doubt not of my love when I am there, all the glory of the place shall never make me forget my business.' When he was on earth, he forgot none of the business for which he came into the world; 'Shall I not do my Father's business?' said he, when he was a child; yes, and he did it to the utmost, by fulfilling all righteousness. Surely therefore he will not forget any of that business which he is to do in heaven, it being the more pleasant work by far. And (as I showed in the former discourse, out of Hebrews 6:20) 'He is entered as a forerunner', an harbinger, to take up places there for us; and if he could forget us, yet our names are all written in heaven round about him, and are continually afore his eyes written there, not only by God's election, 'Ye are come to mount Zion, and to the heavenly Jerusalem, and to the church of the firstborn which are written in heaven, and to Jesus, and to the blood of sprinkling', *etc.* (*Heb.* 12:23–23), but Christ himself scores them up anew with his blood, over every mansion there, which he takes up for any. Yea, he carrieth their names written in his heart, as the high priest did the names of the ten[1] tribes on his breast, when he entered into the holy of holies. He sits in heaven to see to it, that none other should take their rooms over their heads, as we say. And therefore, salvation is said to be 'reserved in heaven for them' (*1 Pet.* 1:4), that is, kept on purpose for them by Jesus Christ. The evil angels had places there once, but they were disposed of unto others over their heads, as the land of Canaan was from the Canaanites; the reason of which was, because they had not a Christ there to intercede for them as we have.

(2.) Then, secondly, to manifest his mindfulness of them, and of all believers else, when he should be in

---

[1] Qu, 'twelve'?—Ed.

his glory, he tells them that when he hath despatched that business for them, and made heaven ready for them, and all the elect that are to come, that then he means to come again to them. So chapter 14, verse 3, 'If I go and prepare a place for you, I will come again', which is a mere expression of love, for he if he had pleased, he might have ordered it to have sent for them to him; but he means to come for them himself, and this when he is warm (as we speak) and in the height and midst of his glory in heaven; yet he will for a time leave it to come again unto his spouse. And what is it for? [1.] To see her, 'I will see you again, and your heart shall rejoice.' [2.] To fetch her, 'I will come again and receive you to myself' (*John* 14:3). He condescends to the very laws of bridegrooms, for notwithstanding all his greatness, no lover shall put him down in any expression of true love. It is the manner of bridegrooms, when they have made all ready in their father's house, then to come themselves and fetch their brides, and not to send for them by others, because it is a time of love. Love descends better than ascends, and so doth the love of Christ, who indeed is love itself, and, therefore comes down to us himself; 'I will come again and receive you unto myself' (says Christ), 'that so where I am, you may be also.' That last part of his speech, gives the reason of it, and withal bewrays his entire affection. It is as if he had said, The truth is, I cannot live without you, I shall never be quiet till I have you where I am, that so we may never part again; that is the reason of it. Heaven shall not hold me, nor my Father's company, if I have not you with me, my heart is so set upon you; and if I have any glory, you shall have part of it. So verse 19, 'Because I live, you shall live also.' It is a reason, and it is half an oath besides, *As I live* is God's oath; *Because I live*, says Christ. He pawns his life upon it, and desires to live upon no other terms, 'He shall live to see his seed', *etc.* (*Isa.* 53). And yet farther, the more to express the workings and longings of his heart after them all that while, he tells them it shall not be long neither ere he doth come again to them. 'Again a little while and ye shall see me; a little while and ye shall not see me,' says he (*John* 16:16). Which not seeing him refers not to that small space of absence whilst dead and in the grave, but of that after his last ascending, forty days after his resurrection, when he should go away, not to be seen on earth again until the day of judgment; and yet from that ascension but 'a little while', says he, 'and you shall see me again', namely, at the day of judgment. It is said, 'Yet a little while, and he that shall come will come, and will not tarry' (*Heb.*

10:37). The words in the Greek are ἔτι γαρ μιχρον ὁσον ὁσον, ὁ ἐρχομενος ἠξει, 'As little little as may be.' Though long for the time in itself, yet as little while as may be in respect of his desire, without the least delaying to come. He will stay not a moment longer, than till he hath despatched all our business there for us. And then the doubling of the phrase, ὁ ἐρχομενος ἠξει, *veniens veniet*, 'Coming he will come', implies vehemency of desire to come, and that his mind is always upon it, he is still a-coming, he can hardly be kept away. Thus the Hebrew phrase likewise signifies an urgency, vehemency, and intenseness of some act, as 'expecting I have expected', 'desiring I have desired', so coming he will come. And as not content with these expressions of desire, he adds over and above all these, 'and will not tarry'; and all to signify the infinite ardency of his mind towards his elect below, and to have all his elect in heaven about him. He will not stay a minute longer than needs must, he tarries only till he hath throughout all ages by his intercession prepared every room for each saint, that he may entertain them all at once together, and have them all about him.

(3.) Thirdly, what his heart would be towards them in his absence he expresseth by the careful provision he makes, and the order he takes for their comfort in his absence, 'I will not leave you as orphans' (so the word is), I will not leave you like fatherless and friendless children, at sixes and sevens (*John* 16:18). My Father and I have but only one friend, who lies in the bosom of us both, and proceedeth from us both, the Holy Ghost, and in the mean time I will send him to you, doing herein as a loving husband useth to do in his absence, even commit his wife to the dearest friend he hath; so doth Christ, verse 16, 'I will pray the Father', says he, 'and he shall give you another Comforter.' And chapter 16:7, he saith, 'I will send him to you.' Who,

First, shall be a better Comforter unto you than I am to be in this kind of dispensation, which whilst I am on earth I am bound up towards you in. So in that 16th of John verse 7 he intimates, 'It is expedient', says he, 'that I go away: for if I go not away, the Comforter will not come', who, by reason of his office, will comfort you better than I should do with my bodily presence. And this Spirit, as he is the 'earnest of heaven', as the apostle speaks, so he is the greatest token and pledge of Christ's love that ever was, and such a one as 'the world cannot receive.' And yet,

Secondly, all the comfort he shall speak to you all that while will be but from the expression of my heart towards you; for as he comes not of himself but I must send him (*John* 16:7), so 'he will speak nothing of himself, but whatsoever he shall hear, that shall he speak' (verse 13). And he says, 'He shall receive of mine, and shall show it unto you' (verse 14). Him, therefore, I shall send on purpose to be in my room, and to execute my place to you, my bride, spouse, and he shall tell you, if you will listen to him, and not grieve him, nothing but stories of my love. So it is there, 'He shall glorify me', namely, to you; for I am in myself already glorified in heaven. All his speech in your hearts will be to advance me, and to greaten my worth and love unto you, and it will be his delight to do it. And he can come from heaven in an instant when he will, and bring you fresh tidings of my mind, and tell you the thoughts I last had of you, even at that very minute when I am thinking of them, what they are at the very time wherein he tells you them. And therefore in that 1 Corinthians 2, by 'having the Spirit' (verse 12), we are said to 'have the mind of Christ' (verse 16); for he dwelleth in Christ's heart, and also ours, and lifts up from one hand to the other what Christ's thoughts are to us, and what our prayers and faith are to Christ. So that you shall have my heart as surely and as speedily as if I were with you; and he will continually be breaking your hearts, either with my love to you, or yours to me, or both; and if either, you may be sure of my love thereby. And whereas, says he, you have the Spirit now in your hearts, so, verse 17 of chapter 14, 'he now dwells in you'; yet after my ascension 'he shall be', in a further measure, 'in you', as it follows there. And at that day, 'you shall know' (namely, by his dictate) 'that I am in my Father, and you in me, and I in you' (verse 20). He will tell you, when I am in heaven, that there is as true a conjunction between me and you, and as true a dearness of affection in me towards you, as is between my Father and me, and that it is as impossible to break this knot, and to take off my heart from you, as my Father's from me, or mine from my Father. And then,

Thirdly, you shall be sure that what he says of my love to you is true, for 'he is the Spirit of truth' chapter 16, verse 13, as also chapter 14, verse 16, 17, which Christ speaks of him as he is a Comforter. And as you believe me when I tell you of my Father, because I come from him, so you may believe him in all that he says of me and of my love to you, for he comes from me.

Aye, but might they say, Will not he also leave us for a time, as you have done? No, says Christ, 'The Father shall give you another Comforter, and he shall abide with you for ever' (14:16). Christ speaks it in opposition to himself. He himself had been a comforter unto them, but he was now to be absent; but not so the Spirit. 'He shall be with you for ever'; and as he is now 'with you', so he 'shall be in you' (verse 17).

In the *fourth* place, if this be not enough to assure them how his heart would be affected towards them, he assures them he will give them daily experience of it. Do but try me, says he, when I am gone, and that by sending me word upon all occasions what you would have me to do for you, and I have left my Spirit to be your secretary and the inditer[1] of all your petitions. 'Hitherto you have asked nothing [that is, little] in my name'—he blames them that they have asked him no more to do for them—'but now ask, and you shall receive.' And if otherwise you will not believe, yet you shall believe your own eyes; ask, and you shall see yourselves answered presently. Believe, and so believe me, says be, 'for the works' sake' (*John* 14:11). He speaks it of the works he would do for them in answer to their prayers when he was gone, which should be as so many epistles of his heart returned in answer unto theirs; for it follows, 'He that believeth on me shall do greater works than I,

[1] Composer or writer.—P.

because I go to my Father' (verse 12), so that it is manifest he speaks of the works done after his ascension. And how were they to get and procure them to be done? By prayer; so it follows, 'And whatsoever you shall ask in my name, that will I do' (verse 13). He speaks it of the time when he is gone. And again he says, 'If you shall ask anything in my name, I will do it' (verse 14). Let me but hear from you, be it every week, every day, every hour, you shall be sure of an answer. 'Open your mouths wide, and I will fill them.' And those your prayers shall be as continual tokens both of your hearts towards me, and my answers shall be the like of mine to you. And because Christ bids them direct (their letters) their prayers, to the Father, only to send them in his name (*John* 16:23), and so they might perhaps not so clearly know and discern that his heart was in the answer to them, but his Father's hand only, therefore he adds twice in the 14th of John, 'I will do it, I will do it.' He speaks like one as forward to do for them, as his Father is, or should be, and as desirous to have them know and take notice of his hand in it. And it is as if he had said, Though you ask the Father in my name, yet all comes through my hands, and 'I will do it'; there must be my hand to the warrant for everything that is done, and my heart shall not be wanting.

In the *fifth* place, yet further to evidence his love, he not only bids them thus pray to him and in his name upon all occasions, but he assureth them that he himself will pray for them. And observe but the manner of his telling them this; it is in the most insinuating, persuasive expressions to convey his heart into them that men use to utter when they would intimate the deepest care and purpose to do a thing. 'At that day [namely, after his ascension] ye shall ask', *etc.*, says he, 'and I say not unto you that I will pray the Father for you' (16:26); no, not I. I mentioned it afore; I will but add this illustration to it. It is such a speech as men use when they would express the greatest reason that another hath to rest confident and assured of their love, 'I do not love you, no, not I.' It is an expressing a thing by its contrary, which is most emphatical. As when we say of a man that hath the greatest good turn done him that can be, You are shrewdly hurt. It is such an expression as Paul used to the Corinthians, I converted your souls when you thought not of it; 'I caught you with guile; forgive me this wrong.' So says Christ here, 'I say not that I will pray for you', when the truth is that it is the chiefest work that he doth in heaven. He lives ever to intercede; as he ever lives, so to intercede ever, and never to hold his peace till sinners are saved. But the work of Christ in heaven is a subject deserves and will take up a distinct and large discourse; I will therefore speak no more of it now, neither will I mention any more particulars out of this his sermon. Read but over those three chapters (the 14th, 15th, and 16th), for in them you have the longest sermon of his that is recorded; and he stood the longest upon this theme of any other, because, indeed, his heart was more in it than in any point that he ever preached on.

Only, if any object and say, He spake all this to his disciples to quiet and pacify them, and so, more in respect to their trouble, than otherwise he would have spoken.

In the *sixth* place, read but the next chapter (the 17th), and you shall see that he presently goes apart and alone to his Father, and speaks over all again unto him that which he had said unto them. He says as much behind their backs *of them* as he had said before their faces *to them*. Read it, and you will find that he was the same absent that [he was when] present with them. He was, therefore, not only hearty in what he had said, but his heart was full of it. That chapter, you know, contains a prayer put up just before his suffering, and there he makes his will and his last request, for in such a style it runs, 'Father, I will' (verse 24), which will he is gone to see executed in heaven. And Arminius said true in that, that this prayer is left us by Christ as a summary of his intercession for us in heaven. He spake as he meant to do in heaven, and as one that had done his work, and was now come to demand his wages; 'I have finished thy work', *etc.,* says he (verse 4). And whereas he speaks a word or two for himself (in the first five verses), he speaks five times as many for them, for all the rest of the chapter is a prayer for them. He useth all kind of arguments to move his Father for his children. 'I have finished the work which thou gavest me to do', says he, and to save them is thy work, which remains to be done for me by thee; and 'they are thine, and thou gavest them me', and I commend to thee but thine own. 'And all mine are thine, and thine are mine.' He insinuates that he of himself had not added a man, but useth all his interest only for those that the Father had given him. And what a motive is this? And he professeth he will not open his mouth for a man more: 'I pray not for the world', says he, I will not open my lips for any one son of perdition; but I employ all my blood, my prayers, and my whole interest with thee but for those thyself hast given me. And, says he, though thou hast given me a personal glory, which I had before the world was, yet there is another glory, which

I account of almost as much, and that is, in their being saved. 'I am glorified in them', says he (verse 10), 'and they are my joy' (verse 13), and therefore I must have them 'with me wherever I am' (verse 24). Thou hast set my heart upon them, and hast loved them thyself as thou hast loved me, and thou hast ordained them to be one in us, even as we are one, and therefore I cannot live long asunder from them; I have thy company, but I must have theirs too; 'I will that they be where I am' (verse 24). If I have any glory, they must have part of it. So it follows in the fore-named verse, 'That they may behold the glory which thou hast given me.' He speaks all this as if he had been then in heaven, and in possession of all that glory; and, therefore, it is an expression of his heart in heaven, which you have very good ground to build upon.

Demonstrations from passages and expressions after his resurrection.

II. These demonstrations have been taken from his carriage and sermon before his death, even at his first breaking of his mind unto his disciples concerning his departure from them. Let us now take a view of our Saviour in his behaviour after his resurrection;

whence a further *indicium*[1] of his heart, how it would stand towards sinners when he should be in heaven, may be taken, and his love demonstrated. For his resurrection was the first step unto his glory, and indeed an entrance into it; when he laid down his body, he laid down all earthly weakness, and passions of flesh and blood. 'It was sown', as ours is, 'in weakness'; but with raising of it up again, he took on him the dispositions and qualifications of an immortal and glorious body, 'it was raised in power'. And 'the days of his flesh', or frail estate, as the author to the Hebrews by way of distinction speaks, were past and over at his resurrection; and the garment of his body was new dyed, and endowed with new qualities; and thereby it was made of a stuff fit to bear and sustain heaven's glory; and therefore, what now his heart upon his first rising shall appear to be towards us, will be a certain demonstration, what it will continue to be in heaven. And to illustrate this the more, consider, that if ever there were a trial taken, whether his love to sinners would continue or no, it was then at his resurrection; for all disciples (especially Peter) had carried themselves the most unworthily towards him in that interim that could be; and this then when he was performing the greatest act of love towards

[1] Sign or token. — P

them, namely, dying for them, that ever was shown by any. And by the way, so God often orders it, that when he is in hand with the greatest mercies for us, and bringing about our greatest good, then we are most of all sinning against him; which he doth, to magnify his love the more. You know how they all forsook him, and in the midst of his agony in the garden, in which he desired their company, merely for a relief unto his sadded spirit, they slept, and lay like so many blocks, utterly senseless of his dolours,[1] which had they any friendly sympathy of, they could never have done; 'Could you not watch with me one hour?' Then you know how foully Peter denied him with oaths and curses; and after that, when he was laid in the grave, they are giving up all their faith in him; 'We trusted it should have been he', say two of them, 'that should have redeemed Israel.' They question whether he was the Messiah or no (*Luke* 24:21). Now when Christ came first out of the other world, from the dead, clothed with that heart and body which he was to wear in heaven, what message sends he first to them? We would all think, that as they would not know him in his sufferings, so he would now be as strange to them in his glory; or at

---

[1] Intense sorrows. — P

least, his first words shall be to rate[1] them for their faithlessness and falsehood. But here is no such matter; for his first word concerning them is, 'Go tell my brethren' *etc.* (*John* 20:17). You read elsewhere, how that it is made a great point of love and condescending in Christ so to entitle them; 'He is not ashamed to call them brethren' (*Heb.* 2:11); surely his brethren had been ashamed of him. Now for him to call them so when he was first entering into his glory, argues the more love in him towards them. He carries it as Joseph did in the height of his advancement, when he first brake his mind to his brethren; 'I am Joseph your brother', says he (*Gen.* 45:4). So Christ says here, Tell them you have seen Jesus their brother; I own them as brethren still. This was his first compellation; but what was the message that he would first have delivered unto them? That I, says he, 'ascend to my Father, and your Father'. A more friendly speech by far, and arguing infinite more love than that of Joseph's did (though that was full of loving affection), for Joseph after he had told them he was their brother, adds, 'whom you sold into Egypt'; he minds them of their unkindness; but not so Christ, not a word of that, he minds them not of what they had done against him. Poor sinners, who are full of

[1] Scold or chide (= 'berate'). —P.

the thoughts of their own sins, know not how they shall be able at the latter day to look Christ in the face when they shall first meet with him. But they may relieve their spirits against their care and fear, by Christ's carriage now towards his disciples, who had so sinned against him. Be not afraid, 'your sins will he remember no more'. Yea further, you may observe, that he minds them, not so much of what he had been doing for them. He says not, Tell them I have been dying for them, or, that they little think what I have suffered for them; not a word of that neither; but still his heart and his care is upon doing more: he looks not backward to what is passed, but forgets his sufferings, as 'a woman her travail, for joy that a man-child is born'. Having now despatched that great work on earth for them, he hastens to heaven as fast as he can to do another. And though he knew he had business yet to do upon earth, that would hold him forty days longer, yet to show that his heart was longing, and eagerly desirous to be at work for them in heaven, he speaks in the present tense, and tells them, 'I ascend'; and he expresseth his joy to be, not only that he goes to 'his Father', but also that he goes to 'their Father', to be an advocate with him for them, of which I spake afore. And is indeed Jesus our brother alive? And doth he call us brethren? And doth he talk thus lovingly of us? Whose heart would not this overcome?

But this was but a message sent his disciples, before he met them; let us next observe his carriage and speech at his meeting together. When he came first amongst them, this was his salutation, 'Peace be to you' (verse 19), which he reiterates (verse 21); and it is all one with that former speech of his used in that his parting sermon, 'My peace I leave with you.' After this he 'breathes on them', and conveys the Holy Ghost in a further measure into them, so to give an evidence of what he would do yet more plentifully in heaven; and the mystery of that his breathing on them was to show that this was the utmost expression of his heart, to give them the Spirit, and that it came from the very bottom of it (as a man's breath doth), as well as that the Holy Ghost proceeds from him, as well as from the Father, which was also the meaning of it. And to what end doth he give them the Spirit? Not for themselves alone, but that they by the gift and assistance of that Spirit might forgive men's sins by converting them to him. 'Whose sins soever ye remit', namely, by your ministry, 'they are remitted to them.' His mind, you see, is still upon sinners, and his care for the conversion of their souls. And therefore in another evangelist, namely, Mark, his last words recorded are these: 'Go ye into all the world, and preach the gospel unto every creature; and he that believeth shall be saved', *etc.* (*Mark* 16:15). And in Luke (24:46, 47), his last words on earth there recorded are, 'Thus it behoved Christ to suffer and to rise . . . that repentance and remission of sins should be preached among all nations', and adds, 'beginning at Jerusalem', where he had been but a few days before crucified. Of all places, one would have thought he would have excepted that, and have charged them to pass by it; but he bids them begin, there. Let them have the first-fruit and benefit by my death, that were the actors in it. And, to that end, he also says, 'Behold I send you the promise of my Father', *etc.,* (verse 49). Another time he appears to two of them, and then indeed he rates them, saying, 'O ye fools, and slow of heart!' but for what is it, but only because they would not believe on him; for no other sin, not for that they had forsaken him; so it follows, 'O ye fools, and slow of heart to believe', *etc.* (*Luke* 24:25), and this because he is glad when we believe (as *John* 11:16). And after that he appears to all the eleven, and upbraids them, the text says, but with what? With their 'unbelief and hardness of heart'; still because they believed not (so verse 14). No sin of theirs troubled him but their unbelief.

Which shows how his heart stands, in that he desires nothing more than to have men believe in him; and this now when glorified. Afterwards he meets with Thomas, and scarce chides him for his gross unbelief, only tells him, it was well that, 'having seen, he believed'; but pronounceth them more 'blessed, who though they have not seen, yet believe'; and so he is reproved (*John* 20:29). Another time he shows himself to his disciples, and particularly deals with Peter, but yet tells him not a word of his sins, nor of his forsaking of him, but only goes about to draw from him a testimony of his love to himself; 'Peter' (says he), 'lovest thou me?' Christ loves to hear that note; full well do those words sound in his ears, when you tell him you love him, though he knows it already; as Peter tells him, 'Thou knowest all things, thou knowest I love thee' (*John* 21:15), and this Christ puts him thrice upon. And what was Christ's aim in drawing this acknowledgment of love from Peter to him, that if he loved him as he professed, and would ever show it, then to 'feed his lambs'? This is the great testimony that he would have Peter to show his love in, when he should be in heaven; and this is the last charge he gives him. Which, how great a testimony is it, to show how his own heart was affected, and what his greatest care was upon! His heart runs altogether upon his lambs, upon souls to be converted. He had said afore, 'Sheep I have which are not of this fold, them I must bring in' (*John* 10:6); and he left his apostles to do it; but this here was a more moving and affectionate expression, for sheep can shift for themselves, but poor little lambs cannot. Therefore Christ says unto Peter, 'Feed my lambs'; even as John, to express the more love unto those he writes to, calls them 'my little children'. And to what end doth the evangelist record these things of him after his resurrection? One of the evangelists that recorded them informs us. In the 20th of John verse 30, it is said, that 'Jesus did many other signs', namely, after his resurrection; for in the midst of the story of those things done after his resurrection he speaks it, 'which are not written in this book', but partly recorded by other evangelists, and partly concealed; 'but these things are written that ye might believe, that Jesus is the Christ', that is, that so you might come to him as to the Messiah, the Saviour of the world; and therefore, the most of the things recorded tend to show Christ's heart and carriage towards sinners, that so we might believe on him, and that 'believing we might have life through his name'.

Demonstrations from passages at and after his ascension into heaven.

III. Let us view him next in his very ascending: his carriage then also will further assure our hearts of this. It is said, 'He lifted up his hands and blessed them' (*Luke* 26:50); and to put the greater emphasis upon it, and that we might the more observe it, as having some great mystery in it, it is added, 'And whilst he blessed them, he was parted from them, and carried up into heaven' (verse 51). This benediction Christ reserved to be his last act; and what was the meaning of it, but (as I have before shown) to bless them, as God blessed Adam and Eve, bidding them 'increase and multiply', and so blessing all mankind that were to come of them. Thus doth Christ, in blessing his disciples, bless all those that shall believe through their word unto the end of the world. I only add this to the illustration of it; this mystery is interpreted by Peter (*Acts* 3:26), when, speaking to the Jews, he says, 'Unto you first, God having raised up his Son Jesus, sent him to bless you' (and how?), 'in turning away every one of you from his iniquities', and so forgiving of them; for 'blessed is the man whose sin is forgiven'. Thus at his ascending.

IV. In the next place, let us consider what Christ did when he was come to heaven and exalted there: how abundantly did he there make good all that he had promised in his last sermon!

For, *first*, he instantly poured out his Spirit, and that 'richly' (as the apostle to Titus speaks), and he 'being by the right hand of God exalted, and having received of the Father the promise of the Holy Ghost, he hath shed forth this which you now see and hear', says the apostle in his first sermon after (*Acts* 2:33). He then received it, and visibly poured him out. So it is said, 'He ascended up on high, and gave gifts unto men . . . for the work of the ministry (*Eph.* 4:8, 15), and for the jointing in of the saints to the increase of the body of Christ' (verse 16), that is, for the converting of elect sinners, and making them saints. And the gifts there mentioned (some of them) remain unto this day, in 'pastors and teachers', *etc.* And this Spirit is still in our preaching and in your hearts, in hearing, in praying, *etc.*, and persuades you of Christ's love to this very day; and is in all these the pledge of the continuance of Christ's love still in heaven unto sinners. All our sermons and your prayers are evidences to you, that Christ's heart is still the same towards sinners that ever it was, for the Spirit that assists in all these comes in his name, and in his stead, and works all by commission from him. And do none of you feel your hearts moved in the preaching of these things, at this and other times? And who is it that moves you? It is the Spirit who speaks in Christ's name from heaven, even as himself is said to 'speak from heaven' (*Heb.* 12:25). And when you pray, it is the Spirit that indites your prayers, and that 'makes intercession for you' in your own hearts (*Rom.* 8:26), which intercession of his is but the evidence and echo of Christ's intercession in heaven. The Spirit prays *in* you, because Christ prays *for* you. He is an intercessor on earth, because Christ is an intercessor in heaven. As he did take off Christ's words, and used the same that he before had uttered, when he spake in and to the disciples the words of life, so he takes off Christ's prayers also when he prays in us; he takes but the words as it were out of Christ's mouth, or heart rather, and directs our hearts to offer them up to God. He also follows us to the sacrament, and in that glass[1] shows us Christ's face smiling on us, and through his face his heart; and thus helping of us to a sight of him, we go away rejoicing that we saw our Saviour that day.

Then, *secondly,* all those works, both of miracles and conversion of sinners, in answer to the apostles'

[1] Mirror. —P.

prayers, are a demonstration of this. What a handful had Peter's first sermon after Christ's ascension, when three thousand souls were converted by it! The apostles (you know) went on to preach forgiveness through Christ, and in his name, and to invite men to him; and what signs and wonders did accompany them, to confirm that their preaching! And all were the fruits of Christ's intercession in heaven. So that what he promised (*John* 14:12), as an evidence of his minding them in heaven, was abundantly fulfilled. They upon their asking did 'greater works than he' (so *Acts* 4:29-30), at the prayers of Peter. And the apostle makes an argument of it, 'How shall we escape', says he, 'if we neglect so great salvation, which at the first began to be spoken by the Lord, and was confirmed unto us by them that heard him, God also bearing them witness, both with signs and wonders and with divers miracles?' *etc.* (*Heb.* 2:3-4). Yea, let me add this, that take also the New Testament, and all the promises in it, and expressions of Christ's love, it was written all since Christ's being in heaven, by his Spirit, and that by commission from Christ, and therefore all that you find therein you may build on as his very heart; and therein see, that what he once said on earth, he repealeth not a word now he is in heaven, his mind continues the same. And the consideration hereof may add a great confirmation to our faith herein.

Thirdly, some of the apostles spake with him since, even many years after his ascension. Thus John and Paul, of which the last was in heaven with him, and they both do give out the same thing of him. Paul heard not one sermon of Christ's (that he knew of) whilst on earth, and received the gospel from no man, apostle or other, but by the immediate revelation of Jesus Christ from heaven, as he speaks (*Gal.* 1:11, 12). But he was converted by Christ himself from heaven, by immediate speech and conference of Christ himself with him, and this long after his ascension. And in that one instance Christ abundantly showed his heart and purpose to continue to all sorts of sinners to the end of the world. Thus in two places that great apostle telleth us; the first is, 1 Timothy 1:18, 'I was a persecutor, a blasphemer', says he, 'but I obtained mercy, and the grace of our Lord', namely, Jesus Christ, 'was exceeding abundant'; and upon this he declares with open mouth, as it were, from Christ's own self, who spake to him from heaven, that this is 'the faithfullest saying' that ever was uttered, 'that Christ came into the world to save sinners, whereof I am chief', says he (verse 15). And to testify that this was the very scope of Christ in thus converting of

Paul himself, and Paul's scope also in that place to Timothy, to show so much, appears by what follows, 'For this cause I obtained this mercy, that in me first Jesus Christ might show forth all longsuffering, for a pattern to all them that should hereafter believe on him unto life everlasting' (verse 16). It is express, you see, to assure all sinners, unto the end of the world, of Christ's heart towards them. This was his drift. 'For this very cause', says Paul.

The second place I allege in proof of this, is the story of Paul's conversion, where he diligently inserts the very words that Christ spake to him from heaven (*Acts* 26:16), which were these, 'I have appeared unto thee for this purpose, to make thee a minister and a witness . . . to send thee to the Gentiles, to open their eyes, and to turn them from darkness to light, and from the power of Satan unto God, that they may receive forgiveness of sins, and an inheritance among them that are sanctified by faith that is in me.' Brethren, these are Christ's words since he went to heaven and he tells Paul he appeared unto him to testify thus much. Thus for Paul's conference with him.

Then again, sixty years after his ascension, did the Apostle John receive a revelation from him, even when all the apostles were dead, for after all their deaths was that book written, and the Revelation is said to be in a more immediate manner 'the revelation of Jesus Christ' (so *Rev.* 1:1), than any other of the apostles' writings; and you read that Christ made an apparition of himself to him, and said, 'I am he that was dead, and am alive for evermore' (1:18). Now let us but consider Christ's last words, in that, his last book, the last that Christ hath spoken since he went to heaven, or that he is to utter till the day of judgment; you have them in the last chapter, verse 16, 'I Jesus have sent mine angel to testify unto you these things in the churches. I am the root and the offspring of David . . . And the Spirit and the bride say, Come. And let him that heareth say, Come. And let him that is athirst come. And whosoever will, let him take of the water of life freely.' They are the latter words I cite this place for. The occasion of these words was this: Christ was now in heaven, and had before promised to come again, and fetch us all to heaven. And in the meantime, mark what an echoing and answering of hearts and of desires there is mutually, between him from heaven and believing sinners from below. Earth calls upon heaven, and heaven calls upon earth, as the prophet speaks. The bride from earth says unto Christ, 'Come to me'; and the Spirit in the saints' hearts below says

'Come' unto him also; and Christ cries out as loud from heaven, 'Come', in answer unto this desire in them; so that heaven and earth ring again of it. 'Let him that is athirst come to me; and let him that will come, come, and take of the waters of life freely.' This is Christ's speech unto men on earth. They call him to come unto earth, to judgment; and he calls sinners to come up to heaven unto him for mercy. They cannot desire his coming to them, so much as he desires their coming to him. Now what is the meaning of this, that upon their calling upon him to come, he should thus call upon them to come? It is in effect as if he had plainly uttered himself thus: I have a heart to come to you, but I must have all you my elect that are to be on earth, come to me first. You would have me come down to you, but I must stay here till all that the Father hath given me be come to me; and then you shall be sure quickly to have me with you. Hereby expressing how much his heart now longs after them. This to be his meaning is evident by the words which he adds, verse 20, 'He which testifies these things', namely, Christ, 'says, Surely I come quickly.' And if we observe how much by the by, as it were, these words of Christ's do come in, it makes them the more remarkable to show his heart in uttering them. This book was intended merely as a prophecy of the times of the gospel until his coming; unto which period of it, when John had brought that prophetic story, he brings in the bride longing for that coming of Christ, 'The bride says, Come.' And no sooner says she so, but Christ by way of retortion doth likewise say 'Come' unto her also; yea, it puts the more observation upon it, that he had uttered the same words before (*Rev.* 21:6), but notwithstanding he will repeat them again, and have them to be his last words. All which shows how much his heart was in this part of the gospel, to invite sinners to him; that now when he is to speak but one sentence more, till we hear the sound to judgment, he should especially make choice of these words. Let them therefore for ever stick with you, as being worthy to be your last thoughts when you come to die, and when you are a-going to him. He speaks indeed something else after them; but that which he says afterwards is but to set a seal unto these words, and to the rest of the Scriptures, whereof this is the chief. And further to show that these words were singled out to be his last, and that he meant to speak no more till the day of judgment, therefore also he adds a curse to him, who should 'add to them, or take from them'. He adds indeed after that another speech, but it is only to ingeminate[1] his willingness to come quickly,

[1] Reiterate.—P.

were all his elect but once come in to him (so verse 20). And all this tends to assure us that this is his heart, and we shall find him of no other mind until his coming again.

And that you may yet the more consider them as thus purposely brought in by him as his last words, to make them stick with us, let me add another observation about them, and that is this, that at another time when he was upon earth, he in like manner singled out these very words (I mean the matter of them) as the conclusion of many days' preaching. Thus, 'In the last day, that great day of the feast, Jesus stood and cried, If any man thirst, let him come to me and drink' (*John* 7:37). These words were spoken on the 'last day of the feast', after which he was to preach no more at that time, and for a good while after, unto them; and he had preached upon all the former days of that feast, as his manner was; and it was 'the great day of the feast', when he had the greatest audience; and you see he chooseth this for his last sentence of that his last sermon then; and when he would give them something at parting, as a *viaticum*,[1] which he would have them carry home with them to feed upon

---

[1] Money and/or provisions for a journey; or possibly Goodwin is referring to the eucharist given by the Roman Catholic Church to those in danger of dying. — P.

above all the rest, these are his words, 'If any man thirst, let him come to me and drink'; which himself interprets to be believing on him (verse 38), and he stands up to speak this; yea, 'he cries', says the text, with open mouth, with utmost vehemency, to the intent that all might hear this above all sayings else. And thus in like manner, at this time also, when he is to speak no more, but to hold his tongue for ever till the day of judgment, nor is to write any more Scriptures, he then sends his angel to testify these to be his last words; and this although he had spoken them before. It was therefore assuredly done to show his heart in them. They were his last words then, and they shall be mine in the closure of this discourse, for what can there be added to them?

PART 2

INTERNAL DEMONSTRATIONS OF THE TENDERNESS OF CHRIST'S HEART TOWARDS SINNERS

For we have not an high priest which cannot be touched with the feeling of our infirmities; but was in all points tempted like as we are, yet without sin.
Hebrews 4:15

THE only use I shall make of these words is, to be a foundation unto that second part of that head or point of doctrine into which I have made an entrance; which was to demonstrate the gracious inclination and temper of Christ's heart toward sinners, now he is in heaven.

II. The extrinsical demonstrations of this, which I make the first part of it, are despatched. And for a

47

groundwork to these more intrinsical demonstrations, which make a second part, I have chosen this text, as that which above any other speaks his heart most, and sets out the frame and workings of it towards sinners; and that so sensibly that it doth, as it were, take our hands, and lay them upon Christ's breast, and let us feel how his heart beats and his affections yearn toward us, even now he is in glory—the very scope of these words being manifestly to encourage believers against all that may discourage them, from the consideration of Christ's heart towards them now in heaven.

To open them, so far as they serve to my present purpose.

First, all that may any way discourage us he here calls by the name of infirmities, thereby meaning both

1. The evil of *afflictions*, of what sort soever, persecutions, *etc.*, from without.

2. The evil of *sins*, which do most of all discourage us, from within.

And that both these are meant,

1. That under 'infirmities' he means persecutions and afflictions is manifest; not only in that the word is often used in that sense (as 2 *Cor.* 11:30; 12:5), but also it is plain that the phrase is here so intended,

for his scope is to comfort them against what would pull from them their profession, as that forego- ing exhortation, 'Let us hold fast our profession', implies. Now that which attempted to pull it from them were their persecutions and oppositions from without. It appears also because his argument here of comforting them against these infirmities, is drawn from Christ's example, 'In that he was in all things tempted as we are.'

2. Yet *secondly,* by 'infirmities' are meant sins also, for so in the process of this discourse he useth the phrase, and makes them the main object of our high priest's pity; for in the next words, chapter 5:2, show- ing what the qualifications of the high priests under the law were, who were types of our great high priest, he makes this one suitable to this here mentioned, that he was to be one that 'could have compassion on the ignorant, and those that were out of the way'; that is, upon sinners, for sins are those ignorances and goings astray from God; and then adds, 'in that himself has clothed with infirmities', that is, with sins. And although it is said here that Christ was without sin in all, yet he was tempted by Satan unto all sorts of sins, even as we are. And that by 'infirmities' sins are mainly here intended, is yet more evident from the remedy propounded against them, which they are

here encouraged to seek for at the throne of grace, namely, grace and mercy. 'Therefore let us come boldly to the throne of grace, that we may find grace and mercy to help in time of need.' So it follows in the next words. Grace to help against the power of sin, and mercy against the guilt and punishment of it; both which are the greatest discouragers to come boldly to that throne; and therefore he must needs intend those kinds of infirmities chiefly in this his encouragement and comfortory[1] given.

Now, *secondly,* for a support against both these, he lets us understand how feelingly and sensibly affected the heart of Christ is to sinners under all these their infirmities, now he is in heaven, for of him advanced into heaven he here speaks, as appeareth by verse 14. And if the coherence with that verse be observed, we shall see that he brings in this narration of it setly,[2] by way of preventing an objection which might otherwise arise in all men's thoughts from that high and glorious description which he had given of him in that 14th verse. 'We have a great high priest, who is passed into the heavens', *etc.* He knew we would be apt from this presently to think, he may be too great to be an high priest for us, to transact our affairs; and

[1] Reassurance.—P.
[2] In a set or fixed way, that is, firmly.—P.

that this greatness of his might cause him to forget us, or, if he did remember us, and take notice of our miseries, yet, 'being passed into the heavens', and so having cast off the frailties of his flesh which he had here, and having clothed his human nature with so great a glory, that therefore he cannot now pity us, as he did when he dwelt among us here below, nor be so feelingly affected and touched with our miseries, as to be tenderly moved to compassionate and commiserate us, so he is not now capable of a feeling of grief, and so not of a fellow-feeling or sympathizing with us; his state and condition now is above all such affections, which affections notwithstanding are they that should put him upon helping us, heartily and cordially. And for him to be exposed to such affections as these, were a weakness, an infirmity in himself, which heaven hath cured him of. His power and glory is so great that he cannot be thus touched, even as the angels are not. And he is 'advanced far above all principalities and powers' (*Eph.* 1:15).

This the apostle carefully pre-occupates;[1] and it is the very objection which he takes away. 'We have not a high priest who cannot', *etc. Duplex negatio œquipollet affirmationi*; nay, two negatives do not only make an affirmative, but affirm more strongly:

---

[1] Anticipates. —P.

they make an affirmation contradictory to a contrary and opposite thought. Now this speech of his is as much as if he should have said, Well, let heaven have made what alteration soever upon his condition, in glorifying his human nature, which be it never so free from fleshly passions, and instead of flesh be made like heaven, let him be never so incapable of impressions from below; yet he retains one tender part and bare place in his heart still unarmed, as it were, even to suffer with you, and to be touched if you be. The word is a deep one, συμπαθησαι. He *suffers with you,* he is as tender in his affections to you as ever he was; that he might be moved to pity you, he is willing to suffer, as it were, one place to be left naked, and to be flesh still, on which he may be wounded with your miseries, that so he might be your merciful high priest.

And whereas it may be objected, that this were a weakness, the apostle affirms that this is his power, and a perfection and strength of love surely, in him, as the word δυναμενον importeth; that is, that makes him thus *able and powerful* to take our miseries into his heart, though glorified, and so to be affected with them, as if he suffered with us, and so to relieve us out of that principle out of which he would relieve himself.

There are two things which this text gives me occasion to take notice of, and apart to handle.

First, more generally, that Christ's heart now in heaven is as graciously affected unto sinners as ever it was on earth.

And, *secondly,* more particularly, the manner how. Or thus

1. That he is touched with a feeling, or sympathises with us, as the word is.

2. The way how this comes to pass; even through his having been tempted in all things like unto us. In handling the first, I shall give those intrinsical demonstrations of it that remain; and in handling the other, further open the text. To come therefore first to those intrinsical demonstrations of this doctrine, which I engraft upon these words, and shoot naturally from them, namely, That the heart of Jesus Christ, now he is in heaven, is as graciously inclined to sinners as ever it was on earth.

The first sort of intrinsical demonstrations, drawn from the influence all the three Persons have for ever into the heart of the human nature of Christ in heaven.

I. The first sort of demonstrations shall be fetched from all the three Persons, and their several influence they have into Christ's heart in heaven, to incline it towards us.

1. The first shall be taken from God his Father, who hath thus advanced him; and it hath two parts: (1.) That God hath given a perpetual command to Christ to love sinners; (2.) That therefore his heart continues the same for ever.

(1.) For the first, God the Father hath given Jesus Christ a special command to love sinners; and hath withal implanted a merciful, gracious disposition in his heart toward them. This I mention to argue it, because it is that which Christ allegeth (*John* 6:37), as the original ground of this disposition of his, 'not to cast out those that come to him'. For 'it is my Father's will', says he in the following verses, 'that I should perform that which I came down from heaven for' (verse 38). And this lies now still upon him, now he is in heaven, as much as ever; for 'his will also is', says he (verses 39, 40), 'that I should raise them up at the last day', so as it must needs continue the same till then. And compare with this the 10th of John, from verse 15 to 18, where, having discoursed before of his care and love to his sheep, to 'give his life' for them, to 'know' and own them, and to 'bring them into the fold', *etc.,* he concludes at verse 18, 'This commandment have I received from my Father.' It is his will, says the 6th of John, and if a good son knows that a thing is his father's mind and will, it is enough to move him to do it; much more if it be his express command. And in this 10th of John, he further says, that it is the command which he had received from the Father. A command is a man's will peremptorily expressed; so as there must be a breach, if it be not fulfilled: and such a command hath God given Christ concerning us. Out of both which places I observe three things to be the matter of this will and command of God's.

First, that Christ should die for his sheep; in respect to which command, he continued so to love them whilst here, as to lay down his life for them (so John 10:15); but then he took it up again, and is ascended into heaven. Therefore, those other two things commanded him, do concern him when he is in glory; namely, to 'receive all that come to him', which is the *second;* and the *third,* to look that he 'lose none of those for whom he died', but to 'raise them up'. And for these his Father's command lies as strictly on him, now he is in heaven, as for dying for them whilst he was on earth. 'This command have I received from my Father, and this is his will.'

And together with this command, God did put it into his heart, as where he commands he ever useth to do, such an instinct of transcendent love towards them, as shall so strongly incline him to perform it, that he shall need no more commands. He hath put such a στοργη, such an *especial love* into him, as he hath put into the hearts of parents towards their own children, more than to all other men's children which they see besides, although more beautiful and more witty[1] than their own. And both this commandment, and this inclination of love towards them, we have at once expressed, Psalm 40:8, where, giving the reason why he became our Mediator and sacrificed himself, he not only says, 'I come to do thy will, O God'; but also, 'Thy law is in my heart.' In which speech, both these two are mentioned:

[1.] That command I mentioned is there expressed, for it is called a law. And,

[2.] It was a law wrought into suitable dispositions in his heart; and, therefore, said to be a 'law in his heart' or affections.

You may easily conceive what law it was by the subject of it, his heart, which is still put for the most tender affections (*Col.* 3:12, 'Bowels of mercy, kindness', *etc.*). It was no other than that law of love, mercy, and pity to poor sinners which God gave him in charge, as he was to be Mediator. It was that

---

[1] Clever, bright. —P.

special law which lay on him as he was the 'second Adam', like that which was given to the first Adam, *non concedendi*,[1] over and above the moral law, not to eat the forbidden fruit; such a law was this he there speaks of. It was the law of his being a Mediator and a sacrifice, for of that he expressly speaks, verses 6, 7, over and besides the moral law, which was common to him with us. The word in the original is, 'In the midst of my bowels', to show it was deeply engraven; it had its seat in the centre, it sat nearest and was most inward in his heart.

Yea, and as that special law of not eating the forbidden fruit was to Adam *præceptum symbolicum*,[2] as divines call it, given over and besides all the ten commandments, to be a trial, a sign or symbol, of his obedience to all the rest, such was this law given unto Christ, the second Adam, so as that God would judge of all his other obedience unto himself by this. Yea, it was laid on him with that earnestness by God, and so commended[3] by him, as that if ever Christ would have him to love him, he should be sure to love us. Thus in that place fore-cited (*John* 10:17, 18), Christ comforts himself with this in his obedience,

---

[1] Latin: not to allow.— P.
[2] Latin: symbolical commandment.—P.
[3] Qu. 'commanded'?—Ed.

'Therefore doth my Father love me.' It is spoken in relation unto his fulfilling this his command formerly mentioned, and so withal imports, as if God should love Christ the better for the love he should show to us, it pleased him so well to see Christ love us. And so it is as if God, when he gave Christ that commandment (verse 18), had said, Son, as you would have my love continue towards you, let me see your love towards me shown in being kind to these I have given you, 'whom I have loved with the same love wherewith I have loved you', as you have it, John 17:23. As God would have us show love unto him by loving his children, so he would have Christ also show his love towards him by loving of us.

(2.) Now, for the *second* branch of this demonstration, namely, that that love which Christ when on earth expressed to be in his heart, and which made him die for sinners upon this command of his Father, that it doth certainly continue in his heart still, now that he is in heaven, and that as quick and as tender as ever it was on earth, even as when he was on the cross, and that because of his Father's command. It is evidenced thus, for it being a law written in the midst of his heart by his Father, it becomes natural to him, and so indelible, and, as other moral laws of God written in the heart are, perpetual. And as in us, when we shall be in heaven, though faith shall fail and hope vanish, yet love shall continue, as the apostle speaks; so doth this love in Christ's heart continue also, and suffers no decay, and is shown as much now in receiving sinners and interceding for them, and being pitiful unto them, as then in dying for them. And this love to sinners being so commanded and pressed upon him, as was said, that as he would have his Father love him, he should love them, and so being urged upon all that great love that is between him and his Father, this, as it must needs work and boil up a strong love in him unto sinners, so likewise the most constant and never-decaying love that could be. And this is argued from the analogy of that principle upon which Christ urgeth us to love himself (*John* 15:10). He moveth his disciples to 'keep the commandments' he gave them, and useth this argument, 'For so shall you abide in my love', and backs it with his own instance, 'Even as I have kept my Father's commandments, and abide in his love.' Now, therefore, this being the great commandment that God layeth on him, to love and die for, and to continue to love and receive, sinners that come to him, and raise them up at the latter day, certainly he continues to keep it most exactly, as being one of the great ties between him and his Father, so to continue in his love to him. Therefore, so long as he continues in his Father's love, and, now he is in heaven and at his right hand, he must needs continue in highest favour with him, so long, you may be sure, he continues to observe this. And thus that he should continue still to love us, both love to his Father and love to himself obligeth him; we may therefore be sure of him, that he both doth it and will do it for ever. O what a comfort is it, that as children are mutual pledges and ties of love between man and wife, so that we should be made such between God the Father and the Son! And this demonstration is taken from the influence of the first person of the Trinity, namely, from God the Father.

2. Then, *secondly,* this his love is not a forced love, which he strives only to bear towards us, because his Father hath commanded him to marry us; but it is his nature, his disposition, which, added to the former, affords a second demonstration of the point in hand, and is drawn from God the Son. This disposition is free and natural to him; he should not be God's Son else, nor take after his heavenly Father, unto whom it is natural to show mercy, but not so to punish, which is his strange work, but mercy pleaseth him; he is 'the Father of mercies', he begets them naturally. Now, Christ is his own Son, ἴδιος υἱός, as by way of distinc-

tion he is called, and his natural Son; yea, his human nature being united to the second person, is thereby become the natural Son of God, not adopted, as we are. And if he be his natural Son in privileges, then also his Father's properties are natural to him, more natural than to us, who are but his adopted sons. And if we, 'as the elect of God', who are but the adopted sons, are exhorted to 'put on bowels of mercy, kindness, humbleness of mind, meekness', *etc.* (as *Col.* 3:12), then much more must these dispositions needs be found in Christ, the natural Son; and these, not put on by him, but be as natural to him as his Sonship is. 'God is love', as John says, and Christ is love covered over with flesh, yea, our flesh. And besides, it is certain that as God hath fashioned the hearts of all men, and some of the sons of men unto more mercy and pity naturally than others, and then the Holy Spirit, coming on them to sanctify their natural dispositions, useth to work according to their tempers, even so it is certain that he tempered the heart of Christ, and made it of a softer mould and temper than the tenderness of all men's hearts put together into one, to soften it, would have been of. When he was to assume a human nature, he is brought in saying, 'A body hast thou fitted me' (*Heb.* 10:5); that is, a human nature, fitted, as in other things, so in the temper of it, for the Godhead to work and show his perfections in best. And as he took a human nature on purpose to be a merciful high priest (as *Heb.* 2:14), so such a human nature, and of so special a temper and frame as might be more merciful than all men or angels. His human nature was 'made without hands'; that is, was not of the ordinary make that other men's hearts are of; though for the matter the same, yet not for the frame of his spirit. It was a heart bespoke for on purpose to be made a vessel, or rather fountain, of mercy, wide and capable enough to be so extended as to take in and give forth to us again all God's manifestative mercies; that is, all the mercies God intended to manifest to his elect. And therefore Christ's heart had naturally in the temper of it more pity than all men or angels have, as through which the mercies of the great God were to be dispensed unto us; and this heart of his to be the instrument of them. And then this man, and the heart of this man so framed, being united to God, and being made the natural Son of God, how natural must mercy needs be unto him, and therefore continue in him now he is in heaven! For though he laid down all infirmities of our nature when he rose again, yet no graces that were in him whilst he was below; they are in him now as much as ever; and being his nature, for nature we know is constant, therefore still remains. You may observe, that when he was upon earth, minding to persuade sinners to have good thoughts of him, as he used that argument of his Father's command given him; so he also lays open his own disposition, 'Come to me, you that are weary and heavy laden, . . . for I am meek and lowly of heart' (*Matt.* 11:28). Men are apt to have contrary conceits of Christ, but he tells them his disposition there, by preventing such hard thoughts of him, to allure them unto him the more. We are apt to think that he, being so holy, is therefore of a severe and sour disposition against sinners, and not able to bear them. No, says he; 'I am meek', gentleness is my nature and temper. As it was of Moses, who was, as in other things, so in that grace, his type; he was not revenged on Miriam and Aaron, but interceded for them. So, says Christ, injuries and unkindnesses do not so work upon me as to make me irreconcilable, it is my nature to forgive: 'I am meek.' Yea, but (may we think) he being the Son of God and heir of heaven, and especially being now filled with glory, and sitting at God's right hand, he may now despise the lowliness of us here below; though not out of anger, yet out of that height of his greatness and distance that he is advanced unto, in that we are too mean for him to marry, or be familiar with.

He surely hath higher thoughts than to regard such poor, low things as we are. And so though indeed we conceive him meek, and not prejudiced with injuries, yet he may be too high and lofty to condescend so far as to regard, or take to heart, the condition of poor creatures. No, says Christ; 'I am lowly' also, willing to bestow my love and favour upon the poorest and meanest. And further, all this is not a semblance of such an affable disposition, nor is it externally put on in the face and outward carriage only, as in many great ones, that will seem gentle and courteous, but there is all this ἐν τη χαρδια, 'in the heart'; it is his temper, his disposition, his nature to be gracious, which nature he can never lay aside. And that his greatness, when he comes to enjoy it in heaven, would not a whit alter his disposition in him, appears by this, that he at the very same time when he uttered these words, took into consideration all his glory to come, and utters both that and his meekness with the same breath. So verse 27, 'All things are delivered to me by my Father'; and presently after all this he says, 'Come unto me, all you that are heavy laden . . . I am meek and lowly' (verses 28, 29). Look, therefore, what lovely, sweet, and delightful thoughts you use to have of a dear friend, who is of an amiable nature, or of some eminently holy or meek saint, of whom you think with yourselves, I could put my soul into such a man's hands, and can compromise my salvation to him, as I have heard it spoken of some. Or look how we should have been encouraged to have dealt with Moses in matter of forgiveness, who was the meekest man on earth; or treated with Joseph, by what we read of his heart towards his brethren, or what thoughts we have of the tender hearts of Paul or Timothy unto the souls of men in begetting, and in nurturing, and bringing them up to life, 'Being affectionately desirous of you, we were willing [says Paul] to impart our own souls to you' (*1 Thess.* 2:8); and this 'naturally', as his word is (*Phil.* 2:20); even such and infinitely more raised apprehensions should we have of that sweetness and candour that is in Jesus Christ, as being much more natural to him.

And therefore the same apostle doth make Christ's bowels[1] the pattern of his, 'God is my witness, how greatly I long after you in the bowels of Jesus Christ' (*Phil.* 1:8). This phrase, 'in the bowels of Christ', hath, according to interpreters, two meanings, and both serve to illustrate that which I intend. *First,* 'in the bowels of Christ' is taken causally, as if he meant to

---

[1] The term 'bowels' has been retained in this section, as Goodwin uses it frequently with reference to the AV usage and explains its meaning (p. 66); see also footnote, p. 3. — P.

show that those bowels or compassions were infused into him from Christ, and so longed after them with such kind of bowels as Christ had wrought in him; and if so that Christ put such bowels into him, hath he not then in himself much more? Paul had reason to say, 'in the bowels of Christ', for (in this sense) I am sure he once had scarce the heart and bowels of a man in him; namely, when he was out of Christ, how furious and lion-like a spirit had he against the saints, and what havoc made he of them, being ready even to pull out their bowels! And how came Paul by such tender bowels now towards them? Who gave him now such tender affections? Even Jesus Christ, it was he that of a lion made him a lamb. If therefore in Paul these bowels were not natural, but the contrary rather were natural to him, and yet they so abounded in him, and that naturally, as himself speaks, how much more must they needs abound in Christ, to whom they are native and inbred? Or else, *secondly*, 'in the bowels', is put for *instar*,[1] 'like the bowels', or 'after the bowels', according to the analogy of this Hebrew phrase. And so then the meaning were this, like as the bowels of Jesus Christ do yearn after you, so do mine. 'Bowels' are a metaphor to signify tender and motherly affections and mercies. So Luke

[1] Latin: likeness or resemblance. — P.

1:78, 'through the tender mercies'. In the original it is 'the bowels of mercy'. Thus Paul, when he would signify how tender his affections were, he instances 'in the bowels of Jesus Christ' (he making Christ his pattern in this in all, 'Be ye followers of me, as I am of Christ'). Now, how desirous was this great apostle to beget men to Christ! He cared not what else he lost, so he might win some. He 'counted not his life dear' nay, not his salvation dear, but 'wished himself accursed for his brethren', who yet were the greatest enemies Christ then had on earth. How glad was he when any soul came in! How sorry when any fell off! Falling 'into a new travail (he knew not how better to express the anxiety of his spirit for the Galatians), 'till Christ was formed in them'. How comforted was he when he heard tidings of the constancy and increase of any of their faith! (*1 Thess.* 3:6, 7); and verse 8 he says, 'for now we live, if you stand fast in the Lord'. Read all his epistles, and take the character of his spirit this way; and when you have done, look up to Christ's human nature in heaven, and think with yourselves, 'Such a man is Christ.' Paul warbles out in all these strains of affections but the soundings of Christ's affections in heaven, in a lower key. They are natural to Christ, they all and infinite more are eminent in him. And this is the second demonstration, taken from his own natural disposition as Son of God.

3. A third demonstration shall be taken from the third person of the Trinity, the Holy Ghost. If the same Spirit that was upon him, and in him, when he was on earth, doth but still rest upon him now he is in heaven, then these dispositions must needs still entirely remain in him.

This demonstration is made up of two propositions put together: (1.) That the Holy Ghost dwelling in him concurs to make his heart thus graciously affected to sinners; and (2.) That the same Spirit dwells and continues in and upon him for ever in heaven.

(1.) For the first: It was the Spirit who overshadowed his mother, and, in the meanwhile, knit that indissoluble knot between our nature and the second person, and that also knit his heart unto us. It was the Spirit who sanctified him in the womb. It was the Spirit that rested on him above measure, and fitted him with a meek spirit for the works of his mediation; and indeed for this very grace sake of meekness did the Spirit come more especially upon him. Therefore, when he was first solemnly inaugurated into that office, at his baptism (for then he visibly and professedly entered upon the execution of it), the Holy Ghost descended upon him; and how? As a dove; so all the evangelists jointly report it. But why in the shape of a dove? All apparitions that God at any time made of himself, were not so much to show what God is in himself, as how he is affected towards us, and declare what effects he works in us. So here, this shape of a dove resting upon him was to show those special gracious dispositions wherewith the Holy Ghost fitted Jesus Christ to be a Mediator. A dove, you know, is the most innocent and most meek creature, without gall, without talons, having no fierceness in it, expressing nothing but love and friendship to its mate in all its carriages, and mourning over it in its distresses; and was therefore a fit emblem to express what a frame and temper of spirit the Holy Ghost did upon this his descending on him, fill the heart of Christ with, and this without measure, that as sweetly as doves do converse with doves, sympathising and mourning each over other, so may we with Christ, for he thus sympathiseth with us. And though he had the Spirit before, yet now he was anointed with him, in respect of such effects as these, which appertained to the execution of his office, with a larger measure and more eminently than before. Therefore the evangelist Luke notes upon it (chapter 4:1), 'Jesus being full of the Holy Ghost, returned from Jordan.' And

Peter also puts the like gloss upon it, as appears (*Acts* 10:37), for speaking there of the baptism of John, he shows how 'after that his being baptized, he began to preach', and 'how God having anointed him with the Holy Ghost', namely, at that baptism of his, 'he went about doing good', *etc.* And that this was the principal thing signified by this descending of the Holy Ghost as a dove upon him, even chiefly to note out his meekness, and sympathising heart with sinners, wrought in him by the Holy Ghost, is evident by two places, where Christ himself puts that very intendment on it.

The first presently after, in the first sermon that he preached after that his having received the Holy Ghost (in the same 4th of Luke), where first it is noted, verse 1, that he returned from being baptized, 'full of the Spirit', and so was led to be tempted; then, verse 14, it is said that he returned from being tempted, 'in the power of that Spirit', and after this is explained by himself, the mystery of his having received the Spirit in the likeness of a dove, and this is the subject matter of the first text which he opened in his first sermon, singled out by him on purpose, by choice, not chance, out of Isaiah, which he read to them (verse 18), 'The Spirit of the Lord is upon me, because he hath anointed me to preach the gospel to the poor', that is, in spirit, the afflicted in conscience for sin; 'he hath sent me to heal the broken-hearted, to preach deliverance to the captives, and recovering sight to the blind, to set at liberty them that are bruised', *etc.* And when he had read so much as concerned the expressing the compassionate disposition of his Spirit unto sinners, whose misery he sets down by all sorts of outward evils, then he reads no further, but closeth the book, as intimating that these were the main effects of that his receiving the Spirit. 'The Spirit of the Lord is upon me, *because* he hath anointed me to preach the gospel to the poor'; that is, for this end, or for this very purpose hath he given me his Spirit, because I was designed or anointed to this work, and by that Spirit also hath he anointed or qualified me with these gifts and dispositions suitable to that work.

Another place that makes the fruit and end of his receiving the Spirit then at his baptism, to be these tender dispositions unto sinners, is that in Matthew 12:18, 19, *etc.*, out of another place in Isaiah, 'Behold my beloved, in whom my soul is well pleased; I will put my Spirit upon him, and he shall show judgments to the Gentiles', *etc.* That seems to be a terrible word, but be not afraid of it, for by 'judgment' is meant even the doctrine of free grace and of the gospel, that changeth and reforms men. As in like manner (according to the Hebrew phrase), in verse 20, by judgment is meant the work of God's grace on men's hearts, when he says, 'He will send forth judgment unto victory', the work of grace being the counterpart of the doctrine of grace. And in preaching this doctrine (which in itself is good tidings) the prophet shows how he should carry it with a spirit, answerable and suitable thereunto, even full of all meekness, stillness, calmness, and modesty, which he expresseth by proverbial speeches usual in those times, to express so much by, 'He shall not strive, nor cry, neither shall any man hear his voice in the streets', that is, he shall deal with all stillness and meekness, without violence or boisterousness. John had the voice of a crier, he was a man of a severe spirit; but Christ came 'piping and dancing', all melodious sweetness was in his ministry and spirit; and, in the course of his ministry, he went so tenderly to work, he was so heedful to broken souls, and had such regard to their discouragements, that it is said he would not 'break a bruised reed', that is, he would set his steps with such heed as not to tread on a reed that was broken in the leaf; or he would walk so lightly or softly, that if it lay in his way, though he went over it, yet he would not have further bruised it: nor quenched either by treading out 'the smoking flax', which is easily done, or with any rushing motion have raised so much wind as to blow out a wick of a candle, as some translate it, smoking in the socket, which the least stirring of the air puffs out. All this is to express the tenderness of his heart; and this, upon his receiving the Spirit, and especially from the time of his baptizing; for then, you know, those words were together therewith uttered, 'This is my beloved Son, in whom I am well pleased'; and they are the same words also, which, together with God's giving him the Spirit, are joined in that 40th of Isaiah, whence these words are taken, so that he was filled with the Spirit, to that end to raise up in him such sweet affections towards sinners.

(2.) Now, for the second part that goes to make up this demonstration: it is as certain that the same Spirit that was upon Christ, and acted[1] his spirit here below, doth still abide upon him in heaven. It must never be said, the Spirit of the Lord is departed from him, who is the sender and bestower of the Holy Ghost upon us. And if the Spirit once coming upon his members 'abide with them for ever', as Christ promiseth (*John* 14:16), then much more doth this Spirit abide upon Christ the Head, from whom we all,

---

[1] That is, 'actuated'.—Ed.

since Christ was in heaven, receive that Spirit, and by virtue of which Spirit's dwelling in him, he continues to dwell in us. Therefore, of him it is said, 'The Spirit of the Lord shall rest upon him' (*Isa.* 11:2). Yea, and in that story of the Holy Ghost's descending upon him at his baptism, it is not only recorded, that 'he descended on him', but over and above it is added, 'and abode upon him'. Yea, further, to put the greater emphasis upon it, it is twice repeated (*John* 1:32), 'I saw the Spirit' (says the Evangelist) 'descending from heaven like a dove'; and he adds this also as a further thing observed by him, 'and it abode upon him'. And then again (verse 38), 'I knew him not' (says he) 'but that he that sent me gave me this token to know him by, upon whom thou shalt see the Spirit descending, and remaining on him, the same is he.' And further, as it is intimated there, he 'rested on him' to that end, that he might baptize us with the Holy Ghost unto the end of the world: 'The same' (says he) 'is he that baptizeth with the Holy Ghost.' He at first descends as a dove, and then abides as a dove for ever upon him; and this dove itself came from heaven first. And therefore, certainly, now that Christ himself is gone to heaven, he abides and sits upon him much more as a dove still there. Moreover, let me add this, that although the Spirit rested on him here without measure in comparison of us, yet it may be safely said, that the Spirit, in respect of his effects in gifts of grace and glory, rests more abundantly on him in heaven, than he did on earth, even in the same sense that at his baptism, as was said, he rested on him in such respects more abundantly than he did before his baptism, during the time of his private life. For as when he came to heaven he was installed king and priest, as it were, anew, in respect of a new execution; so, for the work to be done in heaven, he was anew anointed with this 'oil of gladness above his fellows' (*Psa.* 45:7). Which place is meant of him especially as he is in heaven, at God's right hand, in fulness of joy (*Psa.* 16:11), it is also spoken of him, when also it is, that he 'goes forth in his majesty to conquer', as verse 4 of that 45th Psalm. And yet, then, 'meekness' is not far off, but is made one of his dispositions in his height of glory. So it follows in the fore-cited verse, 'In thy majesty ride prosperously, because of truth and meekness', *etc.* Therefore Peter says (*Acts* 2:36), that 'that same Jesus whom you [Jews] have crucified', and who was risen and ascended, 'God hath made both Lord and Christ': *Lord,* that is, hath exalted him as King in heaven; and *Christ,* that is, hath also anointed him; and this oil is no other than the Holy Ghost, with whom, the same Peter tells us, he was anointed at his baptism (*Acts* 10:38). Yea, and because he then at once received the Spirit in the fullest measure that for ever he was to receive him, therefore it was that he shed him down on his apostles, and 'baptized them with him' (as in that 2nd of the Acts we read). Now it is a certain rule, that whatsoever we receive from Christ, that he himself first receives in himself for us. And so one reason why this oil ran then so plentifully down on the skirts of this our High Priest, that is, on his members the apostles and saints, and so continues to do unto this day, is because our High Priest and Head himself was then afresh anointed with it. Therefore Peter, giving an account how it came to pass that they were so filled with the Holy Ghost, says, that Christ 'having received from the Father the promise of the Holy Ghost, had shed him forth on them' (*Acts* 2:33); which receiving is not to be only understood of his bare and single receiving the promise of the Holy Ghost for us, by having power then given him to shed him down upon them, as God had promised, though this is a true meaning of it; but further, that he had received him first as poured forth on himself, and so shed him forth on them, according to that rule, that whatever God doth unto us by Christ, he first doth it unto Christ. All promises are made and fulfilled unto him first, and so unto us in him; all that he bestows on us he receives in himself. And this may be one reason why (as *John* 7:39) 'the Spirit was not as yet given, because Jesus was not as yet glorified'. But now he is in heaven, he is said to 'have the seven spirits'; so Revelation 1:8, which book sets him out as he is since he went to heaven. Now those seven spirits are the Holy Ghost, for so it must needs be meant, and not of any creature, as appears by the 4th verse of that chapter, where 'grace and peace' are wished 'from the seven spirits'; so called, in respect of the various effects of him both in Christ and us, though but one in person. And seven is a number of perfection, and is therefore there mentioned, to show, that now Christ hath the Spirit in the utmost measure that the human nature is capable of. And as his knowledge (which is a fruit of the Spirit) since his ascension is enlarged—for before he knew not when the day of judgment should be, but now when he wrote this book of the Revelation he did—so are his affections (I speak of the human nature) extended; all the mercies that God means to bestow being now actually to run through his hands, and his particular notice, and he to bestow them, not on the Jews only, but on Gentiles also, who were to be converted after he went to heaven. And so he hath now an heart adequate to

God's own heart, in the utmost extent of showing mercy unto any whom God hath intended it unto.

And this is the third demonstration, from the Spirit's dwelling in him; wherein you may help your faith, by an experiment of the Holy Ghost his dwelling in your own hearts, and there not only working in you meekness towards others, but pity towards yourselves, to get your souls saved; and to that end, stirring up in you incessant and 'unutterable groans' before the throne of grace, for grace and mercy. Now the same Spirit dwelling in Christ's heart in heaven, that doth in yours here, and always working in his heart first for you, and then in yours by commission from him; rest assured, therefore, that that Spirit stirs up in him a heart of mercy infinitely larger towards you than you can have unto yourselves.

A second sort of demonstrations, from several engagements now lying upon Christ in heaven.

II. There are a second sort of demonstrations, which may be drawn from many other several engagements continuing and lying upon Christ now he is in heaven, which must needs incline his heart towards us as much, yea more, than ever. As,

1. The continuance of all those near and intimate

relations and alliances unto us of all sorts, which no glory of his can make any alteration in, and therefore not in his heart and love, nor a declining any respects and offices of love, which such relations do call for at his hands. All relations that are natural, such as between father and child, husband and wife, brother and brother, *etc.*, look what world they are made for, in that world they for ever hold, and can never be dissolved. These fleshly relations, indeed, do cease in that other world, because they were made only for this world; as, 'the wife is bound to her husband but so long as he lives' (*Rom.* 7:1). But these relations of Christ unto us were made in order to 'the world to come', as the Epistle to the Hebrews calls it; and therefore are in their full vigour and strength, and receive their completement therein. Wherefore it is that Christ is said to be 'the same today, yesterday, and for ever' (*Heb.* 13:8). To illustrate this by the constant and indissoluble tie of those relations of this world, whereto no difference of condition, whether of advancement or abasement, can give any discharge. We see in Joseph, when advanced, how as his relations continued, so his affections remained the same to his poor brethren, who yet had injured him, and also to his father. So Genesis 45, where in the same speech he mentioneth both his own greatest dignities and advancement: 'God hath made me a father to Pharaoh, and lord of all his house, and a ruler throughout all the land of Egypt' (verse 8), and yet withal he forgetteth not his relations, 'I am Joseph, your brother' (verse 4), even the same man still. And his affections appeared also to be the same; for he 'wept over them, and could not refrain himself' (verse 1, 2). And the like he expresseth to his father (verse 9), 'Go to my father, and say, Thus saith thy son Joseph, God hath made me lord over all Egypt' (and yet thy son Joseph still).

Take another instance, wherein there was but the relation of being of the same country and alliance, in Esther, when advanced to he queen of an hundred, twenty, and seven provinces; who when she was in the arms of the greatest monarch on earth, and enjoyed highest favour with him, yet then she cries out, 'How can I endure to see the evil that shall come unto my people, or how can I endure to see the destruction of my kindred!' (*Est.* 8:6). She considered but her relation, and how doth it work in her veins by a sympathy of blood! Now much more doth this hold good of husband and wife, for they are in a nearer relation yet. Let the wife have been one that was poor and mean, fallen into sickness, *etc.*, and let the husband be as great and glorious as Solomon in all his royalty, all mankind would cry shame on such a man, if he should not now own his wife, and be a husband in all love and respect to her still. But beyond all these relations, the relation of head and members, as it is most natural, so it obligeth most; 'No man ever yet hated his own flesh', says the apostle, though diseased and leprous, 'but loveth and cherisheth it.' And it is the law of nature, that 'if one member be honoured, all the members are to rejoice with it' (*1 Cor.* 12:26); 'and if one member suffer, all the rest are to suffer with it'. 'Even so is Christ' (verse 12). And these relations are they that do move Christ to continue his love unto us. 'Jesus knowing that he was to depart out of this world, having loved his own who were in the world, he loved them unto the end' (*John* 13:1). And the reason thereof is put upon his relation to them: they were 'his own', and his own by virtue of all relations whatsoever, his own brethren, his own spouse, his own flesh; and 'the very world will love its own', as himself speaks, much more will he himself love his own. 'He that provides not for his own family is worse than an infidel', says the apostle. Now though Christ be in heaven, yet his people are his family still; they are retainers to him, though they be on earth, and this as truly as those that stand about his person now he is in his glory. So that speech evidently declares, 'Of whom the whole family in heaven and earth is named'; they all together make up but one and the same family to him as their Lord. Christ is both the founder, the subject, and the most perfect exemplar and pattern to us, of the relations that are found on earth.

(1.) *First*, he is the founder of all relations and affections that accompany them both in nature and grace. As therefore the Psalmist argues — 'Shall he not see who made the eye?' (*Psa.* 94:9) — so do I. Shall not he who put all these affections into parents and brothers, suitable to their relations, shall not he have them much more in himself? Though our father Abraham, being in heaven, 'be ignorant of us, and Israel acknowledge us not, yet, O Lord, thou art our Father, and our Redeemer', *etc.* (*Isa.* 36:16). The prophet speaks it of Christ, as appears by verses 1 and 2, and in a prophecy of the Jews' call; and he speaks it of Christ, as supposed in heaven, for he adds, 'Look down from heaven, and behold from the habitation of thy holiness and thy glory.' There are but two things that should make him to neglect sinners: his holiness, as they are sinners, and his glory, as they are mean and low creatures. Now he there mentions both, to show that notwithstanding either as they are sinners he rejects them not, and as they are base and mean, he despiseth them not.

(2.) He is the subject of all relations, which no creature is. If a man be a husband, yet not a father, or a brother; but Christ is all, no one relation being sufficient to express his love, wherewith he loveth and owneth us. And therefore he calls his church both sister and spouse (*Song of Sol.* 5:1).

(3.) He is the pattern and exemplar of all these our relations, and they all are but the copies of his. Thus, in Ephesians 5, Christ is made the pattern of the relation and love of husbands. 'Husbands', says the apostle, 'love your wives, as Christ loved his church' (verse 25). Yea, verses 31–33, the marriage of Adam, and the very words he then spake of cleaving to a wife, are made but the types and shadows of Christ's marriage to his church. Herein I speak, says he, 'concerning Christ and the church, and this is a great mystery.' *First*, a mystery; that is, this marriage of Adam was ordained hiddenly, to represent and signify Christ's marriage with his church. And *secondly*, it is a great mystery, because the thing thereby signified is in itself so great, that this is but a shadow of it. And therefore all those relations, and the affections of them, and the effects of those affections, which you see and read to have been in men, are all, and were ordained to be, as all things else in this world are, but shadows of what is in Christ, who alone is the truth and substance of all similitudes in nature, as well as the ceremonial types.

If, therefore, no advancement doth or ought to alter such relations in men, then not in Christ. 'He is not ashamed to call us brethren' (*Heb.* 2:11). And yet the apostle had just before said of him, verse 9, 'We see Jesus crowned with glory and honour.' Yea, and as when one member suffers the rest are touched with a sympathy, so is it with Christ. Paul persecuted the saints, the members, and 'Why persecutest thou me?' cries the Head in heaven; the foot was trodden on, but the Head felt it, though 'crowned with glory and honour'. 'We are flesh of his flesh, and bone of his bone' (*Eph.* 5:30); and therefore as Esther said, so says Christ, 'How can I endure to see the evil that befalls my people?' If a husband hath a wife that is mean, and he become a king, it were his glory, and not his shame, to advance her; yea, it were his shame to neglect her, especially if, when the betrothment was first made, she was then rich and glorious, and a king's daughter, but since that fallen into poverty and misery. Now, Christ's spouse, though now she be fallen into sin and misery, yet when she was first given to Christ by God the Father, who from all eternity made the match, she was looked upon as all glorious; for in election at first both Christ and we were by God considered in that glory which he means to bring him and us unto at last, that being first in God's intention, which is last in execution. For God at the beginning doth look at the end of his works, and at what he means to make them; and so he then, primitively intending to make us thus glorious, as we shall be, he brought and presented us to his Son in that glass of his decrees under that face of glory wherewith at last he meant to endow us. He showed us to him as apparelled with all those jewels of grace and glory which we shall wear in heaven. He did this then, even as he brought Eve unto Adam, whose marriage was in all the type of this; so that as this was the first idea that God took us up in, and that we appeared in before him, so also wherein he presented us then to Christ, and as it were said, Such a wife will I give thee; and as such did the second person marry us, and undertook to bring us to that estate. And that God ordained us thus to fall into sin and misery was but to illustrate the story of Christ's love, and thereby to render this our lover and husband the more glorious in his love to us, and to make this primitive condition whereunto God meant again to bring us the more eminently illustrious; and, therefore, we being married unto him, when we were thus glorious in God's first intention, although in his decrees about the execution of this, or the bringing us to this glory, we fall into meanness and misery before we attain to it, yet the marriage still holds. Christ took us to run the same fortune with us, and that we should do the like with him; and hence it was, that we being fallen into sin, and so our flesh become frail and subject to infirmities, that he therefore 'took part of the same' (*Heb*. 2:14). And answerably on the other side, he being now advanced to the glory ordained for him, he can never rest till he hath restored us to that beauty wherein at first we were presented to him, and till he hath purged and 'cleansed us, that so he may present us to himself a glorious church' (*Eph*. 5:26, 27), even such as in God's first intention we were shown to him to become, having that native and original beauty, and possessing that estate, wherein he looked upon us when he first took liking to us and married us. This is argued there from this very relation of his being our husband (verses 25–26); and, therefore, though Christ be now in glory, yet let not that discourage you, for he hath the heart of a husband towards you, being 'betrothed unto you for ever in faithfulness and in lovingkindness' (*Hos*. 2:19), and the idea of that beauty is so imprinted on his heart, which from everlasting was ordained you, that he will never cease to sanctify and to cleanse you till he hath restored you to that beauty which once he took such a liking of.

2. A second engagement. This love of his unto us is yet further increased by what he both did and suffered for us here on earth before he went to heaven. 'Having loved his own' so far as to die for them, he will certainly 'love them unto the end', even to eternity. We shall find in all sorts of relations, both spiritual and natural, that the having done much for any beloved of us doth beget a further care and love towards them; and the like effect those eminent sufferings of Christ for us have certainly produced in him. We may see this in parents, for besides that natural affection planted in mothers towards their children, as they are theirs, the very pains, hard labour, and travail they were at in bringing them forth, increaseth their affections towards them, and that in a greater degree than fathers bear; and, therefore, the eminency of affection is attributed unto that of the mother towards her child, and put upon this, that it is 'the son of her womb' (*Isa.* 49:15). And then the performing of that office and work of nursing them themselves, which yet it is done with much trouble and disquietment, doth in experience yet more endear

those their children unto them, which they so nurse to an apparent difference of affection and love, in comparison of that which they put forth to others of their own children which they nursed not; and, therefore, in the same place of Isaiah, as the mother's affection to 'the son of her womb', so to her 'sucking child' is mentioned as being the highest instance of such love. And as thus in paternal affection, so also in conjugal, in such mutual loves in the pursuing of which there have any difficulties or hardships been encountered; and the more those lovers have suffered the one for the other, the more is the edge of their desires whetted and their love increased, and the party for whom they suffered is thereby rendered the more dear unto them.

And as it is thus in these natural relations, so also in spiritual. We may see it in holy men, as in Moses, who was a mediator for the Jews, as Christ is for us, Moses therein being but Christ's type and shadow, and therefore I the rather instance in him. He under God had been the deliverer of the people of Israel out of Egypt with the hazard of his own life, and had led them in the wilderness, and given them that good law that was their wisdom in the sight of all the nations, and by his prayers kept off God's wrath from them. And who ever, of all those heroes we read of, did so much for any nation, who yet were continually murmuring at him, and had like once to have stoned him? And yet what he had done for them did so mightily engage his heart, and so immovably point and fix it unto their good, that although God in his wrath against them offered to make of him alone a greater and mightier nation than they were, yet Moses refused that offer, the greatest that ever any son of Adam was tempted with, and still went on to intercede for them, and, among other, used this very argument to God, even the consideration of what he had already done for them, as 'with what great might and power he had brought them out of Egypt', *etc.*, thereby to move God to continue his goodness unto them (*Exod.* 32:11, and elsewhere). And this overcame God, as you may read in the 14th verse of the forenamed chapter. Yea, so set was Moses his heart upon them, that he not only refused that former offer which God made him, but he made an offer unto God of himself to sacrifice his portion in life for their good: 'Rather', says he, 'blot me out of the book of life' (verse 32).

And we may observe the like zealous love in holy Paul, towards all those converts of his whom in his epistles he wrote unto; towards whom that which so much endeared his affections was the pains, the cost, the travail, the care, and the sufferings that he had had in bringing them unto Christ. Thus, towards the Galatians how solicitous was he! how afraid to lose his labour on them! 'I am afraid of you, lest I have bestowed upon you labour in vain': so he expresseth himself (*Gal.* 4:11); and he utters himself yet more deeply, 'My little children (says he), of whom I again travail in birth, until Christ be formed in you' (verse 19). He professeth himself content to be in travail again for them, rather than lose that about which he had been in travail for them once before.

Now from both these examples, whereof the one was Christ's type, and the other the very copy and pattern of Christ's heart, we may raise up our hearts to the persuasion of that love and affection which must needs be in the heart of Christ, from that which he hath done and suffered for us.

First, for Moses; did Moses ever do that for that people which Christ hath done and suffered for you? He acknowledged that he had 'not borne that people in his womb'; but Christ bare us all, and we were the 'travail of his soul', and for us he endured the birth-throes of death (as Peter calls them, *Acts* 2:24). And then for Paul, 'Was Paul crucified for you?' (says Paul likewise of himself). But Christ was, and he speaks it the more to enhance the love of Christ.

Or if Paul had been crucified, would or could it have profited us? No. If therefore Paul was contented to have been in travail again for the Galatians, when he feared their falling away, then how doth Christ's heart work much more toward sinners! he having put in so infinite a stock of sufferings for us already, which he is loath to lose, and hath so much love to us besides, that if we could suppose that otherwise we could not be saved, he could be content to be in travail again, and to suffer for us afresh. But he needed to do this but once, as the apostle to the Hebrews speaks, so perfect was his priesthood. Be assured then, that his love was not spent or worn out at his death, but increased by it. His love it was that caused him to die, and to 'lay down his life for his sheep'; and 'greater love than this hath no man', said himself before he did it. But now, having died, this must needs cause him from his soul to cleave the more unto them.

A cause or a person that a man hath suffered much for, according to the proportion of his sufferings, is one's love and zeal thereunto; for these do lay a strong engagement upon a man, because otherwise he loseth the thanks and the honour of all that is already done and passed by him. 'Have you suffered so many things in vain?' says the apostle to the Galatians (3:4), where he makes a motive and an incitement of it, that seeing they had endured so much for Christ, and the profession of him, they would not now lose all for want of doing a little more. And doth not the same disposition remain in Christ? Especially seeing the hard work is over and despatched which he was to do on earth; and that which now remains for him to do in heaven is far more sweet and full of glory, and as the 'reaping in joy', of what he had here 'sown in tears'. If his love was so great, as to hold out the enduring so much; then now when that brunt[1] is over, and his love is become a tried love, will it not continue? If when tried in adversity (and that is the surest and strongest love), and the greatest adversity that ever was; if it then held, will it not still do so in his prosperity much more? Did his heart stick to us and by us in the greatest temptation that ever was; and will his glorious and prosperous estate take it off, or abate his love unto us? Certainly no. 'Jesus the same today, yesterday, and for ever' (*Heb.* 13:8). When he was in the midst of his pains, one for whom he was then a-suffering, said unto him, 'Lord, remember me when thou comest into thy kingdom'; and could Christ mind him then? as you know he did, telling him, 'This day shalt thou be with me in

---

[1] Crisis or shock. —P.

92

paradise.' Then surely when Christ came to paradise he would do it much more; and remember him too, by the surest token that ever was, and which he can never forget, namely, the pains which he was then enduring for him. He remembers both them and us still, as the prophet speaks of God. And if he would have us 'remember his death till he comes', so to cause our hearts to love him, then certainly himself doth it in heaven much more. No question but he remembers us, as he promised to do that good thief, now he is in his kingdom. And so much for this second engagement.

3. A third engagement is the engagement of an office which still lies upon him, and requires of him all mercifulness and graciousness towards sinners that do come unto him. And therefore whilst he continues in that place, and invested with that office, as he for ever doth, his heart must needs continue full of tenderness and affection. Now that office is the office of his priesthood, which this text mentions as the foundation of our encouragement to 'come boldly to the throne of grace, for grace and mercy . . . seeing we have a great high priest entered into the heavens'. Two things I am to show to make up this demonstration.

First, that this office of high priesthood is an

office erected wholly for the showing of grace and mercy.

And *secondly*, that this office doth therefore lay upon Christ a duty to be in all his dispensations full of grace and mercy, and therefore his heart remains most certainly suited and framed thereunto.

For the *first*. The office of high priesthood is altogether an office of grace. And I may call it the *pardon-office*, set up and erected by God in heaven; and Christ he is appointed the lord and master of it. And as his kingly office is an office of power and dominion, and his prophetical office an office of knowledge and wisdom, so his priestly office is an office of grace and mercy. The high priest's office did properly deal in nothing else. If there had not been a mercy-seat in the holy of holies, the high priest had not at all been appointed to have gone into it. It was mercy, and reconciliation, and atonement for sinners that he was to treat about, and so to officiate for at the mercy-seat. He had had otherwise no work, nor anything to do when he should come into the most holy place. Now this was but a typical allusion unto this office of Christ's in heaven. And therefore the apostle (in the text), when he speaks of this our high priest's being entered into heaven, he makes mention of a throne of grace, and this in answer to that in the type both of the high priest of old, and of the mercy-seat in the holy of holies. And further to confirm this, the apostle goes on to open that very type, and to apply it unto Christ, unto this very purpose which we have now in hand. And this in the very next words to my text, chapter 5, 1st, 2nd, and 3rd verses; in which he gives a full description of a high priest, and all the properties and requisites that were to be in him, together with the eminent and principal end that that office was ordained for. Now the great and essential qualifications there specified, that were to be in a high priest, are mercy and grace, and the ends for which he is there said to be ordained are works of mercy and grace. And besides what the words in their single standing do hold forth to this purpose, observe that they come in to back and confirm that exhortation in the text, wherein he had set forth Christ as an 'high priest touched with the feeling of infirmities': and that therefore we should 'come with boldness for grace and mercy'; 'for every high priest (says he) taken from among men, is ordained for men in things pertaining to God: that he may offer both gifts and sacrifices for sin'. 'One who can have compassion', *etc*. So that these words are a confirmation of what he had before said, and do set out Christ the substance, in his grace and mercifulness, under Aaron and his sons the shadows; and all this for the comfort of believers.

Now for the ends for which those high priests were appointed, they speak all nothing but grace and mercy unto sinners; it is said, he was one 'ordained for men, to offer both gifts and sacrifices for sins'. There is both the *finis cujus*, the end for whom, and the *finis cui*, the end for which, he was ordained.

(1.) For *whom*. He was ordained for *men*, that is, for men's cause, and for their good. Had it not been for the salvation of men, God had never made Christ a priest. So that he is wholly to employ all his interest and power for them for whose cause he was ordained a priest, and that in all things that are between God and them. He is to transact τα προς τον Θεον, all things that are to be done by us towards God, or for us with God, he is to take up all our quarrels with God, and to mediate a reconciliation between us and him. He is to procure us all favour from God, and to do all that which God would have done for our salvation. And that he might do this willingly, kindly, and naturally for us, as every high priest was 'taken from among men', so was Christ, that he might be a priest of our own kind, and so be more kind unto us, than the nature of an angel could have been. And how much this conduceth to his being a merciful high priest, I shall show anon.

(2.) The *end* for which every high priest was ordained, shows this; he was to 'offer gifts and sacrifices for sins': sacrifices for sins, to pacify God's wrath against sin, and gifts to procure his favour. You know the apostle, in the foregoing words, had mentioned grace and mercy, and encouraged us to come with boldness unto this high priest for both; and answerably to encourage us the more, he says, the high priest by his office was to offer for both: gifts for to procure all grace, and sacrifices to procure all mercy for us, in respect of our sins. Thus you see the ends which he is ordained for are all matter of grace and mercy, and so of encouragement unto men for the obtaining of both, verse 1.

(3.) The *qualification* that was required in a high priest was, that he should be 'one that could have compassion', *etc.*, and this is set forth, verse 2. He that was high priest was not chosen into that office for his deep wisdom, great power, or exact holiness; but for the mercy and compassion that was in him. That is it which is here made the special, and therefore the only mentioned, property in a high priest as such; and the special essential qualification that was inwardly and internally to constitute him and fit him for that office: as God's appointment did outwardly and externally, as verse 4 hath it. And the word δυναμενος, 'that can' or 'is able', imports an inward faculty, a spirit, a disposition, a heart that knows how to be compassionate. And it is the same word that the apostle had before used to express Christ's heart by, even in the words of the text, δυναμενον συμπαθησαι, that is 'who can be touched with the feeling of our infirmities'. And he had also used it of him afore that, in the point of mercy (2:18), δυναται, *etc.*, 'he is able' to succour, *etc.*, which is not meant of any external power (which we usually call ability), but of an internal touch in his will; he hath a heart able to forgive, and to afford help.

Now, therefore, if this be so essential a property to a high priest as such, then it is in Christ most eminently. And as Christ had not been fit to have been God's king, if he had not had all power and strength in him, which is essential to constitute him a king, so not to have been God's high priest, if he had not had such a heart for mercifulness; yea, and no longer to have been a priest than he should continue to have such a heart. Even as that which internally qualifies a minister for the ministry is his gifts, which if he loseth, he is no longer to be in that office; or as reason makes a man a man, which if he loseth he becomes a beast; thus no longer should Christ continue to be a priest than he hath a heart that 'can have compassion', as this second verse hath it. And the word which we translate 'to have compassion', is exceeding emphatical, and the force of it observable; it is in the original μετριοπαθειν, and signifies 'to have compassion according to everyone's measure and proportion'. He had said of Christ in the words of my text, that he was 'touched with the feeling of our infirmities', or that 'he had a suffering with us in all our evils'; and the word also here used imports a suffering.

But then, some greatly distressed souls might question thus: Though he pities me, and is affected, yet my misery and sins being great, will he take them in to the full, lay them to heart, to pity me according to the greatness of them? To meet with this thought therefore, and to prevent even this objection about Christ's pity, the apostle sets him out by what was the duty of the high priest, who was his shadow; that he is one that 'can have compassion according to the measure of every one's distress'; and one that considers every circumstance in it, and will accordingly afford his pity and help, and if it be great, he hath a great fellow-feeling of it, for he is a great high priest. Thy misery can never exceed his mercy. The word here used comes from μετρον, a *measure*, and παθειν, to *suffer*. And that it is the apostle's scope to hold this forth in this word, is evident by what follows, for he on purpose makes mention of those several degrees, proportions, and ranks of sinners under the old law, who were capable of mercy and compassion, 'who can have compassion' (says he) 'on the ignorant, and on them that are out of the way'. In the old law you may read of several degrees and kinds of sinners, for which God appointed or measured out differing and proportionable sacrifices (*Lev.* 4:2, 5), and another for sins against knowledge, or such as were, wittingly committed (6:2, 3, compared with verse 6). Now when any sinner came to the high priest to make atonement for him, the priest was wisely to consider the kind and proportion of his sin; as whether it were a sin of mere ignorance, or whether it were against knowledge; and accordingly he was to proportion a sacrifice, and to mediate for him. And so he did μετριοπαθειν, 'pity him according to measure', or according to reason or discretion, as in the margin it is varied. And therefore the apostle here mentions both the ignorant, that is, those that sin out of mere ignorance, and them that are gone out of the way, namely, by wilful and witting iniquity. And so by this property that was to be in the high priest, doth he here set forth Christ. As the measure of any man's need and distress is from sin and misery, accordingly is he affected towards him. And as we have sins of several sizes, accordingly hath he mercies, and puts forth a mediation proportionable; whether they be ignorances, or sins of daily incursion, or else sins more gross and presumptuous. And therefore let neither of them discourage any from coming unto Christ for grace and mercy.

So that (for the closure of this) here is both the qualification disposing him for this office, merciful compassionateness; and here are the ends of this office, even to deal mercifully with all sorts of sinners, according to the proportion and measure of their sins and miseries. From each of which do arise these corollaries, which make up the demonstration in hand, as the conclusion: 1. That he is no longer fit for this place, than he continues to be of a gracious disposition, and one that can have compassion. 2. That he can no longer be faithful in the discharge of this office, according to the ends for which it was appointed, than he shows all grace and mercy unto them that come unto his throne of grace for it.

And that is the second thing which I at first propounded: that this office did lay a duty upon him to have compassion; and it necessarily follows from the former. And answerably to confirm this, we have both these two brought to our hands in one place together, and which is a parallel place to this last interpreted. It is Hebrews 2:17, 'That he might be a merciful and a faithful high priest', *etc.* He is at once here said to be both merciful and faithful; and both are attributed to him, in respect of this high priest's office, 'faithful high priest'; and that, as it is to be executed in heaven, after the days of his flesh ended. For the apostle giving the reason of it, and showing what it is that fits him to be such a high priest, adds (verse 28), 'in that himself *hath* suffered'; so that it relates to the time after his sufferings ended. Now in that he is said to be merciful, this relates to that internal disposition of his heart, before spoken of, qualifying him for this office; and in that he is said to be faithful, that respects his execution of it; he is faithful in the discharge of the duty which that place lays on him.

So then this goes further than the former, for it shows, that to exercise mercy is the duty of his place, and that, if he will be faithful, he must be merciful. For faithfulness in any office, imports an exact performance of something appointed by him, who designs one to that office, and that as a duty; and that this is a true description of faithfulness, and also that this faithfulness so described is in Christ, we have at once implied, in that which immediately follows in the beginning of the 3rd chapter, verse 3, 'Who was' (says the apostle, going on to speak of Christ) 'faithful to him that appointed him, as Moses also was faithful in all his house'; we have the same thing as expressly spoken in that fore-quoted place (*Heb.* 5), in the next words to those we even now opened (verse 3), 'And by reason hereof he ought to offer for sins.' He speaks it of Christ's type, the high priest (as the former also he had done), but thereby to show that it is Christ's duty also to mediate for all that come to him, 'He ought to do it.' Now then to enforce this consideration, for the help of our faith herein. If this office doth by God's appointment thus bind him to it, and if it be the duty of his place, then certainly he will perform it most exactly, for else he doth not do his duty. And our comfort may be, that his faithfulness lies in being merciful; therefore, you see, they are both here joined together. Every one is to do the proper duty of his place, and exactly to see to that. And therefore the apostle (*Rom.* 12), exhorting to the discharge of the duties of each office in the church (verse 7), he says, 'Let him that hath a ministry', committed to him, 'wait on his ministry'; and, among others, if his place of ministration be to 'show mercy' (verse 8) (which was an office in the church, upon which lay the care of the poor and sick), he is to 'do it with cheerfulness'. And so says Christ of himself (*Isa.* 61:1, 2), 'The Spirit of the Lord is upon me, to bind up the broken-hearted, to open the prison doors to them that are bound', to visit and relieve them, and 'to preach good tidings to the meek'. Such kind of souls are they that he hath the charge of. He is the great shepherd and bishop of souls (*1 Pet.* 2:25), and the sick, and the broken, they are his sheep, his charge, his diocese, as Ezekiel hath it (34:16). And to tend such as these, he looks for ever upon it as his duty, as his own expression upon the like occasion importeth, 'Other sheep I have' (says Christ), 'them I must bring', *etc.* (*John* 10:16). Observe how he puts a με δει, an *I must* upon it; looking at it as his duty, strictly laid upon him by his place of being a shepherd. And the proper duty of his place being to show mercy, he doth it with cheerfulness, as the apostle speaks. For mercy makes one do what they do with cheerfulness. And Christ, as he is the bishop, so the διακονος, the deacon also (for he bears all offices to his church), as of the circumcision, so of the uncircumcision also; so he is called (*Rom.* 15:8). And these offices of high priest, shepherd, bishop, *etc.*, he hath still in heaven; for 'he continues a priest for ever' (*Heb.* 7:24).

Now, therefore, to conclude this head. Never fear that Christ's great advancement in heaven should any whit alter his disposition; for this his very advancement engageth him the more. For although he be 'entered into the heavens', yet consider withal that it is here added, to be an high priest there; and so long fear not, for his place itself will call for mercy from him unto them that treat with him about it. And although in the heavens he be 'advanced far above all principalities and powers', yet still his high priesthood goes with him, and accompanies him; for 'such an high priest became us, as was higher than the heavens' (*Heb.* 7:26). And further, though he sits at God's right hand, and on his Father's throne, yet that throne it is a 'throne of grace', as the text hath it, upon which he sits. And as the mercy-seat in the type was the farthest and highest thing in the holy of holies, so the throne of grace (which is an infinite encouragement unto us) is the highest seat in heaven. So that if Christ will have and keep the greatest place in heaven, the highest preferment that heaven itself can bestow upon him, it engageth him unto grace and mercy. The highest honour there hath this attribute of grace annexed to it in its very title,

'A throne of grace'; and as Solomon says, 'A king's throne is established by righteousness', it continues firm by it, so is Christ's throne by grace. Grace was both the first founder of his throne, or his raiser to it, and also it is the establisher of it.

First, it is the founder of it; for the reason why God did set him up in that place was, because he had more grace and mercy in his heart than all the creatures had, or could be capable of. All favourites are usually raised for something that is eminent in them, either beauty, pleasantness of wit, state policy, or the like. Now if you ask what moved God to advance Christ to this high throne, it was his grace. So Psalm 45:8, 'Grace is poured into thy lips', and so dwells much more in his heart: 'therefore God hath blessed thee'; so it follows, namely, with all those glories in heaven, which are God's blessings to his Son.

And then, *secondly*, grace is the upholder of his throne (*Psa.* 45:4), 'In thy majesty . . . prosper thou', as well 'because of meekness' as of 'righteousness', and also because of 'truth'; that is, the word of truth, 'the gospel of our salvation', as Paul exegetically expoundeth it (*Eph.* 1:13). These are the pillars and supporters of his throne and majesty. And there are two of them, you see, that are of grace (meekness, and the gospel of our salvation), unto one of justice, or righteousness, and yet that one is for us too. And these establish Christ's throne. So it follows (verse 6), 'Thy throne, O God, is for ever and ever', and you know who applies this unto Christ (*Heb.* 1:8). Fear not then, whenas meekness supports his majesty, and grace his throne, and whenas he holds his place by showing these. And thus much from that office that is laid upon Christ as he is a priest.

4. A fourth engagement, which added to the former may mightily help our faith in this, is, his own interest, both in that our salvation is the purchase of his blood, and also that his own joy, comfort, happiness, and glory are increased and enlarged by his showing grace and mercy, in pardoning, relieving, and comforting his members here on earth, under all their infirmities. So that, besides the obligation of an office undertaken by him for us, there is the addition of a mighty interest of his own, coincident therewith, to fix his heart unto faithfulness for us, in all that doth concern us. We see that advocates and attorneys who plead for others, although that they have no share in the estate for which they plead, no title to, or interest therein, yet when they have undertaken a client's cause (if honest), how diligent will they be to promote and carry it for that their client, simply because it is their office, and the duty of their place; and yet they

have but a very small fee given them, in comparison of that estate which ofttimes they follow suit about. How much more would their diligence be whetted, if the lands and estates they sue for were their own, or a purchase of theirs for their wives' jointure, or children's portions! Now such is the pardoning of our sins, the salvation of our souls, and the conforming of our hearts unto Christ; these are the purchase of Christ's blood, and whilst he is exercised in promoving[1] these, he doth good to his own child and spouse, *etc.*, which is in effect a doing good unto himself. Yea, to do these, bringeth in to himself more comfort and glory than it procures to them. And therefore the apostle, in the beginning of the following chapter (namely, *Heb.* 3) says, that Christ is engaged to faithfulness in the execution of his office, not as a mere servant only, who is betrusted by his master, but as an owner, who hath an interest of possession in the things committed to his care, and a revenue from these. So (verse 5), 'Moses verily' (says he) 'was faithful as a servant in God's house, but Christ as a Son over his own house', that is, as an heir of all, 'whose house (or family) are we', says the apostle (verse 6); If a physician for his fee will be faithful, although he be a stranger, much more will he be so

---

[1] Promoting.—P.

if he be father to the patient, so as his own life and comfort are bound up in that of the child's, or when much of his estate and comings in are from the life of the party unto whom he ministers physic.[1] In such a case they shall be sure to want for no care and cost, and to lack no cordials that will comfort them, no means that will cure them and keep them healthful, and no fit diet that may nourish and strengthen them; as the care of that prince of the eunuchs, in the first of Daniel, was, to have those children committed to his charge, to eat and drink of the best, because that on their looks and good liking his place depended. Now so God hath ordered it, even for an everlasting obligation of Christ's heart unto us, that his giving grace, mercy, and comfort to us, is one great part of his glory, and of the revenue of his happiness in heaven, and of his inheritance there.

First, to explain how this may be, consider, That the human nature of Christ in heaven hath a double capacity of glory, happiness and delight; one on that mere fellowship and communion with his Father and the other persons, through his personal union with the Godhead. Which joy of his in this fellowship, Christ himself speaks of (*Psa.* 16:11), as to be enjoyed by him, 'In thy presence is fulness of joy and at thy

---

[1] Medicine. —P.

right hand are pleasures for evermore.' And this is a constant and settled fulness of pleasure, such as admits not any addition or diminution, but is always one and the same, and absolute and entire in itself; and of itself alone sufficient for the Son of God, and heir of all things to live upon, though he should have had no other comings in of joy and delight from any creature. And this is his natural inheritance.

But God hath bestowed upon him another capacity of glory, and a revenue of pleasure to come in another way, and answerably another fulness, namely, from his church and spouse, which is his body. Thus Ephesians 1, when the apostle had spoken the highest things of Christ's personal advancement in heaven that could be uttered, as of his 'sitting down at God's right hand, far above all principalities and powers', *etc.* (verses 20, 21); yet (verse 22) he adds this unto all, 'and gave him to be an head to the church, which is his body, the fulness of him who filleth all in all'. So that although he of himself personally be so full, the fulness of the Godhead dwelling in him, that he overflows to the filling all things; yet he is pleased to account—and it is so in the reality—his church, and the salvation of it, to be another fulness unto him, super-added unto the former. As Son of God he is complete, and that of himself; but as an head, he yet hath another additional fulness of joy from the good and happiness of his members. And as all pleasure is the companion, and the result of action, so this ariseth unto him, from his exercising acts of grace, and from his continual doing good unto, and for those his members; or, as the apostle expresseth it, from his filling them with all mercy, grace, comfort, and felicity, himself becoming yet more full, by filling them; and this is his inheritance also, as that other was. So as a double inheritance Christ hath to live upon: one personal, and due unto him, as he is the Son of God, the first moment of his incarnation, ere he had wrought any one piece of work towards our salvation; another acquired, purchased, and merited by his having performed that great service and obedience; and, certainly, besides the glory of his person, there is the glory of his office of mediatorship, and of headship to his church. And though he is never so full of himself, yet he despiseth not this part of his revenue that comes in from below. Thus much for explication.

Now, secondly, for the confirmation and making up the demonstration in hand. This superadded glory and happiness of Christ is enlarged and increased still, as his members come to have the purchase of his death more and more laid forth upon them; so as when their sins are pardoned, their hearts more sanctified, and their spirits comforted, then comes he to see the fruit of his labour, and is comforted thereby, for he is the more glorified by it, yea, he is much more pleased and rejoiced in this than themselves can be. And this must needs keep up in his heart his care and love unto his children here below, to water and refresh them every moment (see *Isa.* 27:3). For in thus putting forth acts of grace and favour, and in doing good unto them, he doth but good unto himself, which is the surest engagement in the world. And therefore the apostle exhorts men to love their wives upon this ground, that in so doing they love themselves: 'So ought men to love their wives, as their own bodies: he that loveth his wife loveth himself' (*Eph.* 5:28), so strict and near is that relation. Now, the same doth hold true of Christ in his loving his church. And therefore in the same place the love of Christ unto his church is held forth as the pattern and exemplar of ours, 'Even as Christ also loved the church' (verse 25). And so it may well be argued thence, by comparing the one speech with the other, that Christ in loving his church doth but love himself; and then the more love and grace he shows unto the members of that his body, the more he shows love unto himself. And accordingly it is further added there (verse 27), that he daily 'washeth and cleanseth his church', that is, both from the guilt and power of sin, 'that he might present it to himself a glorious church, not having spot or wrinkle', *etc.* Observe, it is to himself. So that all that he doth for his members is for himself, as truly, yea, more fully, than for them; and his share of glory out of theirs is greater than theirs, by how much the glory of the cause is greater than that of the effect. And thus indeed the Scripture speaks of it, as whilst it calls the saints the 'glory of Christ' (2 *Cor.* 8:23). And Christ (*John* 17:13, 22, 23) says, that he is 'glorified in them'. And Psalm 45, where Christ is set forth as Solomon in all his royalty and majesty; yet (verse 11) he is said 'greatly to desire or delight in the beauty' of his queen, that is, the graces of the saints; and that not with an ordinary delight, but he 'greatly desires'; his desire is increased as her beauty is. For that is there brought in as a motive unto her to be more holy and conformed unto him, 'to incline her ear, and forsake her father's house' (verse 10). 'So shall the king greatly desire thy beauty.' Christ hath a beauty that pleaseth him as well as we have, though of another kind; and therefore ceaseth not till he hath got out every spot and wrinkle out of his spouse's face, as we heard the apostle speak even now, 'so to present her glorious unto himself', that is, delightful and pleasing in his eye. And suitably unto this, to confirm us yet more in it, Christ in that sermon which was his solemn farewell before his going to heaven, assures his disciples that his heart would be so far from being weaned from them, that his joy would still be in them, to see them prosper and bring forth fruit (*John* 15:9-11), where his scope is to assure them of the continuance of his love unto them when he should be gone, 'As my Father hath loved me, so have I loved you: continue in my love', *etc.* (verses 9, 10). As if he had said, Fear not you my love, nor the continuance of it in my absence; but look you to do your duty, *etc.* And to give them assurance of this, he further tells them, that even when he is in heaven, in the greatest fulness of pleasure at God's right hand, yet even then his joy will be in them, and in their well-doing, 'These things have I spoken unto you, that my joy may remain in you, and that your joy may be full' (verse 11). He speaks just like a father that is taking his leave of his children, and comforting them at his departure, and giving them good counsel to take good courses when he is gone from them, to keep his commandments, and to love one another (verses 10 & 12), and backs it with this motive, so shall my joy remain in you: it is as fathers use to speak; and it will be for your good too, your joy will be also full.

To open which words a little: the word *remain*, used concerning their abiding in his love, and his joy abiding in them, is used in reference to the continuing of both these towards them in heaven. And when Christ says, 'that my joy may remain in you', it is as if he had said, that I may even in heaven have cause to rejoice in you when I shall hear and know of you, that you agree and are loving each to other, and keep my commandments. The joy which he there calls his joy, '*my* joy' is, not to be understood *objective*, of their joy in him, as the object of it; but *subjective*, of the joy that should be in himself, and which he should have in them. So Augustine long since interpreted it. *Quidnam*, says he, *est illud gaudium Christi in nobis, nisi quod ille dignatur gaudere de nobis?* What is Christ's joy in us, but that which he vouchsafeth to have of and for us? And it is evident by this, that otherwise, if it were their joy which he meant in that first sentence, then that other that follows, 'and your joy shall be full', were a tautology. He speaks therefore of his joy and theirs, as of two distinct things; and both together were the greatest motives that could be given to encourage and quicken his disciples in obedience. Now, take an estimate of

Christ's heart herein, from those two holy apostles Paul and John, who were smaller resemblances of this in Christ. What, next to immediate communion with Christ himself, was the greatest joy they had to live upon in this world, but only the fruit of their ministry, appearing in the graces both of the lives and hearts of such as they had begotten unto Christ? See how Paul utters himself (*1 Thess.* 2:19), 'What is our hope', says he, 'or joy, or crown of rejoicing? Ye are our glory and our joy' (verse 20). And in the 3rd Epistle of John, verse 3, John says the like, that he greatly rejoiced of that good testimony he had heard of Gaius; for, says he, 'I have no greater joy than to hear that my children walk in the truth' (verse 4). Now what were Paul and John but instruments by whom they believed and were begotten? and not on whom. Neither of these were crucified for them; nor were these children of theirs the travail of their souls. How much more then unto Christ, whose interest in us and our welfare is so infinitely much greater, must his members be his joy and his crown? And to see them to come in to him for grace and mercy, and to walk in truth, rejoiceth him much more; for he thereby sees of the travail of his soul, and so is satisfied. Certainly what Solomon says of parents (*Prov.* 10:1), that 'a wise son maketh a glad father', *etc.*, is much more true of Christ. Holiness, and fruitfulness, and comfortableness in our spirits while we are here below, do make glad the heart of Christ, our 'everlasting Father'. Himself hath said it, I beseech you believe him, and carry yourselves accordingly. And if part of his joy arise from hence, that we thrive and do well, then doubt not of the continuance of his affections; for love unto himself will continue them towards us, and readiness to embrace and receive them when they come for grace and mercy.

5. There is a fifth engagement, which his very having our nature, which he still wears in heaven, and which the end or intention which God had ordained Christ's assuming it, do put upon him for ever. For one great end and project of that personal union of our nature unto the Godhead in the second Person for ever, was, that he might be a merciful high priest. So that as his office lays it as a duty upon him, so his becoming a man qualifies him for that office and the performance of it, and so may afford a further demonstration of the point in hand. This we find both to have been a requisite in our high priest, to qualify him the better for mercy and affection; and also one of those great ends which God had in that assumption of our nature.

First, a requisite, on purpose to make him the

more merciful. So, Hebrews 5:1, the place even now insisted on, when yet this primary qualification I then passed over, and reserved unto this mention, it is said, 'Every high priest taken from among men is ordained for men', and that to this end, 'that so he might be one that can have compassion': namely, with a pity that is natural and kindly, such as a man bears to one of his own kind. For otherwise the angels would have made higher and greater high priests than one of our nature; but then they would not have pitied men, as men do their brethren, of the same kind and nature with them.

And *secondly*, this was also God's end and intention in ordaining Christ's assumption of our nature, which that other place before cited, namely, Hebrews 2:16-17, holds forth, 'Verily he took not on him the nature of angels, but the seed of Abraham': that is, an human nature, and that made, too, of the same stuff that ours is of, and 'it behoved him to be made like us in all things, that he might be a merciful high priest', *etc.*, ἵνα ἐλεήμων γένηται, 'to the end he might become', or 'be made merciful'.

But was not the Son of God as merciful (may some say) without the taking of our nature, as afterwards, when he had assumed it? Or is his mercy thereby made larger than of itself it should have been, had he not took the human stature on him?

I answer, Yes; he is as merciful, but yet,

[1.] Hereby is held forth an evident demonstration (and the greatest one that could have been given unto men) of the everlasting continuance of God's mercies unto men, by this, that God is for everlasting become a man; and so we thereby assured that he will be merciful unto men, who are of his own nature, and that for ever. For as his union with our nature is for everlasting, so thereby is sealed up to us the continuation of these his mercies, to be for everlasting; so that he can and will no more cease to be merciful unto men, than himself can now cease to be a man; which can never be. And this was the end of that assumption.

[2.] But, secondly, that was not all. His taking our nature not only adds unto our faith, but some way or other even to his being merciful. Therefore it is said, 'that he might be made merciful', *etc.* That is, merciful in such a way as otherwise God of himself had never been; namely, even as a man. So that this union of both natures, God and man, was projected by God to make up the rarest compound of grace and mercy in the result of it that ever could have been, and thereby fully fitted and accommodated to the healing and saving of our souls. The greatest of that mercy that was in God, that contributes the stock and treasury of those mercies to be bestowed on us: and unto the greatness of these mercies nothing is or could be added by the human nature assumed; but rather Christ's manhood had all his largeness of mercy from the Deity. So that, had he not had the mercies of God to enlarge his heart towards us, he could never have held out to have for ever been merciful unto us. But then, this human nature assumed, that adds a new way of being merciful. It assimilates all these mercies, and makes them the mercies of a man; it makes them human mercies, and so gives a naturalness and kindness unto them to our capacities. So that God doth now in as kindly and as natural a way pity us, who are flesh of his flesh, and bone of his bone, as a man pities a man, thereby to encourage us to come to him, and to be familiar with God, and treat with him for grace and mercy, as a man would do with a man; as knowing that in that man Christ Jesus (whom we believe upon) God dwells, and his mercies work in and through his heart in a human way.

I will no longer insist upon this notion now, because I shall have occasion to touch upon it again, and add unto it under that next third general head, of showing the way how Christ's heart is affected towards sinners. Only take we notice what comfort this may afford unto our faith, that Christ must cease to be a man if he continue not to be merciful; seeing the very plot of his becoming a man was, that he might be merciful unto us, and that in a way so familiar to our apprehensions, as our own hearts give the experience of the like, and which otherwise, as God, he was not capable of. And add but this bold word to it, though a true one, that he may now as soon cease to be God as to be a man. The human nature, after he had once assumed it, being raised up to all the natural rights of the Son of God; whereof one (and that now made natural unto him) is to continue for ever united. And he may as soon cease to be either as to be ready to show mercy. So that not only the scope of Christ's office, but also the intention of his assuming our nature, doth lay a farther engagement upon him, and that more strong than any or than all the former.

PART 3

CHRIST'S AFFECTIONATE COMPASSION FOR SINNERS IN THEIR INFIRMITIES

For we have not an high priest who cannot be touched with the feeling of our infirmities, but was in all things tempted like as we are, yet without sin.
Hebrews 4:15.

*S*OME *generals to clear how this is to be understood, that Christ's heart is touched with the feeling of our infirmities, together with the way how our infirmities come to be feelingly let into his heart.*

I. Having thus given such full and ample demonstrations of the tenderness and sameness of Christ's heart unto us now he is in heaven, with that which it was whilst he was here on earth; and those, both

123

extrinsical (in the first part) and intrinsical (in the second); I now come to the last head which I propounded in the opening of these words, namely, the way and manner of Christ's being affected with pity unto us; both how it is to be understood by us, and also how such affections come to be let into his heart, and therein to work these deep feelings of compassion unto us. This in the beginning of the *second part* I propounded to be handled, as being necessary both for the opening and clearing the words of the text, which mainly holds forth this, as also for the clearing of the thing itself, the point in hand. For, as I there shewed, these words come in by way of preoccupation or prevention of an objection, as if his state now in heaven were not capable of such affection as should tenderly move him to pity and commiseration, he being now glorified both in soul and body. Which thought, because it was apt to arise in all men's minds, the apostle therefore forestalls it, both by affirming the contrary, 'We have not an high priest that cannot be touched', *etc.*, that is, he both *can be*, or is capable of it, and likewise *is* touched, notwithstanding all his glory, as also by his annexing the reason of it, or shewing the way how it comes to pass, in that 'in all points he was tempted like as we are'.

Now in handling and opening these, which is a matter full of difficulty, I shall, with all wariness, proceed to the discovery of what manner of affection in Christ this is, and that by these steps and degrees.

1. This affection of compassion, or his being 'touched with the feeling of our infirmities', is not wholly to be understood in a metaphorical or a similitudinary sense, as those speeches used of God in the Old Testament are to be understood, when 'bowels of compassion' are attributed unto him, and his bowels are said to be 'rolled together', or as whenas it is said of God, that he repented, and was afflicted in all his people's afflictions. All which expressions were of God (as we all know) but merely καθ' ἀνθρωπωπαθειαν, after the manner of men; so to convey and represent to our apprehensions, by what affections use to be in parents or friends in such and such cases (what provoke them unto such and such actions), which like effects proceed from God towards us when he sees us in distress. And so they are spoken rather *per modum effectus*, than *affectus*, rather by way of like effect, which God produceth, than by way of such affection in God's heart, which is not capable of any such passions as these are. Now towards the right understanding of this, the first thing which I affirm is, that barely in such a sense as this, that which is

here spoken of Christ, is not to be understood, and my reason for it is grounded upon these two things put together. *First*, that this affection of his towards us here spoken of, is manifestly meant of his human nature, and not of his Godhead only, for it is spoken of that nature wherein he once was tempted as we now are. So expressly in the next words, which can be meant of no other than his human nature.

And *secondly*, that those kind of expressions which were used of God before the assumption of our nature, only in a way of metaphor and similitude, 'after the manner of men', should in no further or more real and proper sense be spoken of Christ and his human nature now assumed, and when he is a man as truly and properly as we are, I cannot imagine; when I consider and remember that which I last insisted on, that one end of Christ's taking a human nature, was 'that he might be a merciful high priest for ever', in such a way as, he being God alone, could not have been. I confess I have often wondered at that expression there used, 'He took the seed of Abraham, that he might be made a merciful high priest' (*Heb.* 2), which at the first reading sounded as if God had been made more merciful by taking our nature. But this solved the wonder, that this assumption added a new way of God's being merciful, by means of which it may now be said, for the comfort and relief of our faith, that God is truly and really merciful, as a man. And the consideration of this contributes this to the clearing of the thing in hand, that whereas God of himself was so blessed and perfect, that his blessedness could not have been touched with the least feeling of our infirmities, neither was he in himself capable of any such affection of pity or compassion: 'He is not as a man, that he should pity or repent', *etc*. He can indeed do that for us in our distress, which a man that pities us useth to do; but the affections and deep feelings of compassion themselves he is not capable of. Hence, therefore, amongst other ends of assuming man's nature, this fell in before God as one, that God might thereby become loving and merciful unto men, as one man is to another. And so, that what before was but improperly spoken, and by way of metaphor and similitude, in the Old Testament, so to convey it to our apprehensions, might now be truly attributed unto him in the reality; that God might be for ever said to be compassionate as a man, and to be touched with a feeling of our infirmities as a man. And thus by this happy union of both natures, the language of the Old Testament, uttered only in a figure, becomes verified and fulfilled in the truth of it, as in all other things the shadows of it were in

Christ fulfilled. And this is the first step towards the understanding of what is here said of Christ, taken from this comparison with the like attributed unto God himself.

2. A second and further step to let in our understanding to the apprehension of this, is by the like further comparison to be made with the angels, and those affections of love and pity that are certainly found in them. In comparison of which, these affections in Christ's human nature, though glorified, must needs be far more like to ours, even more tender, and more human; for in that Hebrews 2 it is expressly said, 'He therefore took not the nature of the angels, that he might be a merciful high priest.' Part of the intendment of those words is to show and give the reason, not only why he took our nature under frail flesh, though that the apostle mentions (ver. 14), but why a human nature for the substance of it, and not the nature of angels; because in his affections of mercy he would for ever come nearer to us, and have such affections, and of the same kind with ours. Whereas otherwise, in other respects, an angel would have been a higher and more glorious high priest than a man.

Now the angels being fellow-servants with us, as the angel called himself (*Rev.* 22:9), they have affections towards us more assimilated unto ours than God hath, and so are more capable of such impressions from our miseries than God is. Although they be spirits, yet they partake of something analogical, or resembling and answering to those affections of pity, grief, *etc.*, which are in us. And indeed, so far as these affections are seated in our souls, and not drenched in the passions of the body, unto which our souls are united, they are the very same kind of affections in us that are in them. Hence the same lusts that are in men are said to be in devils (*John* 8:44), and therefore the devils also are said to fear and tremble, *etc.* And so, oppositely, the same affections that are in men, so far as they are spiritual, and the spirit or soul is the seat of them, they must needs be found in the good angels. But Christ having a human nature, the same for substance that ours is, consisting both of soul and body, although through glory made spiritual, yet not become a spirit; 'A spirit hath not flesh and bones, as ye see me have', says Christ of himself, after his resurrection (*Luke* 24:39); therefore he must needs have affections towards us, yet more like to those of ours than those are which the angels have. So then by these two steps we have gained these two things, that even in Christ's human nature, though glorified, affections of pity and compassion are true and real,

THE HEART OF CHRIST

and not metaphorically attributed to him as they are unto God; and also more near and like unto ours here than those in the angels are; even affections proper to man's nature, and truly human. And these he should have had, although this human nature had, from the very first assumption of it, been as glorious as it is now in heaven.

3. But now, thirdly, add this further, that God so ordered it, that before Christ should clothe this his human nature with that glory he hath in heaven, and put this glory upon it, he should take it as clothed with all our infirmities, even the very same that doth cleave unto us, and should live in this world, as we do, for many years. And during that time God prepared for him all sorts of afflictions and miseries to run through, which we ourselves do here meet withal; and all that time he was acquainted with, and inured unto, all the like sorrows that we are; and God left him to that infirmity and tenderness of spirit, to take in all distresses as deeply as any of us (without sin), and to exercise the very same affections under all these distresses that we at any time do find stirring in our hearts. And this God thus ordered, on purpose thereby to fit him and to frame his heart, when he should be in glory, unto such affections as these spoken of in the text. And this both this text

suggests to be God's end in it, as also that fore-mentioned place (*Heb.* 2:13), 'Forasmuch as we', namely, his members, 'are partakers of flesh and blood', which phrase doth ever note out the frailties of man's nature (as *1 Cor.* 15:50, *etc.*), 'he himself took part of the same . . . that he might be a merciful high priest', *etc.* (ver. 17). And then the apostle gives this reason for it (ver. 18), 'For in that himself hath suffered, being tempted, he is able'—this ability is, as was before interpreted, the having an heart fitted and enabled, out of experience, to pity—and 'to succour them that are tempted'. The meaning of which is, that it is not the bare taking of a human nature, if glorious from the first, that would thus fully have fitted him to be affectionately pitiful out of experience, though, as was said, the knowledge of our miseries taken in thereby would have made him truly and really affectionate towards us, with affections human and proper to a man, and so much nearer and liker ours than what are in the angels themselves, or than are attributed to God, when he is said to pity us; but further, his taking our nature at first clothed with frailties, and living in this world as we, this hath for ever fitted his heart by experience to be in our very hearts and bosoms; and not only or barely to know the distress, and as a man to be affected with a human affection to one of his kind, but experimentally remembering the like in himself once. And this likewise the text suggests as the way whereby our distresses are let into his heart the more feelingly, now he is in heaven. 'We have not an high priest that cannot be touched with the feeling of our infirmities, but was in all points tempted like as we are, yet without sin.' And the more to comfort us herein, observe how fully and universally the apostle speaks of Christ's having been tempted here below. First, for the matter of them, or the several sorts of temptations, he says he was tempted κατα παντα, 'in all points', or things of any kind, wherewith we are exercised. Secondly, for the manner, he adds that too, καθ ὁμοιοτητα, 'like as we are'. His heart having been just so affected, so wounded, pierced, and distressed, in all such trials as ours use to be, only without sin, God, on purpose, left all his affections to their full tenderness, and quickness of sense of evil. So that Christ took to heart all that befell him as deeply as might be; he slighted no cross, either from God or men, but had and felt the utmost load of it. Yea, his heart was made more tender in all sorts of affections than any of ours, even as it was in love and pity; and this made him 'a man of sorrows', and that more than any other man was or shall be.

Now therefore, to explicate the way how our miseries are let into his heart, and come to stir up such kindly affections of pity and compassion in him, it is not hard to conceive from what hath now been said, and from what the text doth further hint unto us.

(1.) The understanding and knowledge of that human nature hath notice and cognisance of all the occurrences that befall his members here. And for this the text is clear; for the apostle speaks this for our encouragement, that 'Christ is touched with the feeling of our infirmities;' which could not be a relief unto us, if it supposed not this, that he particularly and distinctly knew them; and if not all as well as some, we should want relief in all, as not knowing which he knew, and which not. And the apostle affirms this of his human nature, as was said, for he speaks of that nature that was tempted here below. And, therefore, 'the Lamb that was slain', and so 'the man Christ Jesus' is (*Rev.* 5:6) said to have 'seven eyes', as well as 'seven horns', which seven eyes are 'the seven spirits sent forth into all the earth'. His eyes of providence, through his anointing with the Holy Ghost, are in all corners of the world, and view all the things that are done under the sun. In like manner he is there said to have seven horns for power, as seven eyes for knowledge; and both are defined to be seven, to shew the perfection of both, in their extent reaching unto all things. So that, as 'all power in heaven and earth' is committed unto him as Son of man, as the Scripture speaks, so all knowledge is given him of all things done in heaven and earth, and this as Son of man too; his knowledge and power being of equal extent. He is the Sun as well in respect of knowledge as of righteousness, and there is nothing hid from his light and beams, which do pierce the darkest corners of the hearts of the sons of men. He knows the sores, as Solomon expresseth it, and distresses of their hearts. Like as a looking-glass made into the form of a round globe, and hung in the midst of a room, takes in all the species of things done or that are therein at once, so doth the enlarged understanding of Christ's human nature take in the affairs of this world, which he is appointed to govern, especially the miseries of his members, and this at once.

(2.) His human nature thus knowing all — 'I know thy works, thy labour, and thy patience', *etc. (Rev. 2:2)* — he therewithal hath an act of memory, and recalls how himself was once affected, and how distressed whilst on earth, under the same or the like miseries. For the memory of things here below remains still with him, as with all spirits in either of those two other worlds, heaven or hell. 'Son, remember thou in thy lifetime receivedst thy good things, and Lazarus evil', *etc.*, says Abraham to the soul of Dives in hell (*Luke* 15:25). 'Remember me when thou comest into, thy kingdom', said the good thief to Christ; and, Revelation 1, 'I am he', says Christ, 'that was dead, and am alive.' He remembers his death still, and the sufferings of it; and as he remembers it, to put his Father in mind thereof, so he remembers it also, to affect his own heart with what we feel. And his memory presenting the impression of the like now afresh unto him, how it was once with him; hence he comes feelingly and experimentally to know how it is now with us, and so affects himself therewith; as Dido in Virgil—'*Haud ignara mali, miseris succurrere disco.*'[1] Having experience of the like miseries, though a queen now, I know how to succour those that are therein. As God said to the Israelites when they should be possessed of Canaan their own land (*Exod.* 23:9), 'Ye know the hearts of strangers, seeing ye were strangers', *etc.*, and therefore doth command them to pity strangers, and to use them well upon that motive, so may it be said of Christ, that he doth know the hearts of his children in misery, seeing himself was once under the like. Or, as the apostle exhorts

---

[1] Latin: Not unacquainted with evil, I learn to help the unfortunate.

the Hebrews, 'Remember them that are in bonds, as bound with them, and them that suffer adversity, as being yourselves in the body' (*Heb.* 13:3), and so ere you die, may come to suffer the like. So Christ, the head of the body, which is the fountain of all sense and feeling in the body, doth remember them that are bound and in adversity, having himself been once in the body, and so he experimentally compassionates them. And this is a further thing than the former. We have gained this further, that Christ hath not only such affections as are real and proper to a human nature, but such affections as are stirred up in him, from experience of the like by himself once tasted in a frail nature like unto ours. And thus much for the way of letting in all our miseries into Christ's heart now, so as to strike and affect it with them.

A more particular disquisition, what manner of affection this is; the seat thereof, whether in his spirit or soul only, or the whole human nature. — Some cautions added.

II. But concerning this affection itself of pity and compassion, fellow-feeling and sympathy, or suffering with (as the text calls it), which is the product, result, or thing produced in his heart by these, there still remains another thing more particularly to be inquired into, namely, what manner of affection this is; for that such an affection is stirred up in him, besides and beyond a bare act of knowledge or remembrance how once it was with himself, is evident by what we find in the text. The apostle says, not only that he remembers how himself was tempted with the like infirmities that we are, though that be necessarily supposed, but that he is struck and touched with the feeling of our infirmities; to the producing of which this act of remembrance doth but subserve. And he tells us, Christ is able, and his heart is capable of thus being touched. And the word συμπαθησαι is a deep word, signifying to suffer with us until we are relieved. And this affection, thus stirred up, is it which moveth him so cordially to help us.

Now, concerning this affection, as here thus expressed, how far it extends, and how deep it may reach, I think no man in this life can fathom. If *cor regis*, the heart of a king, be inscrutable, as Solomon speaks, the heart of the King of kings now in glory is much more. I will not take upon me to 'intrude into things which I have not seen', but shall endeavour to speak safely, and therefore warily, so far as the light of Scripture and right reason shall warrant my way.

I shall set it forth three ways

1. Negatively; 2. positively; 3. privatively.

1. *Negatively*—It is certain that this affection of sympathy or fellow-feeling in Christ is not in all things such a kind of affection as was in him in the days of his flesh. Which is clear, by what the apostle speaks of him and of his affections then (*Heb.* 5:7), 'Who in the days of his flesh, when he had offered up prayers and supplications, with strong cryings and tears, was heard in that which he feared.' Where we see his converse and state of life here below, to be called by way of difference and distinction from what is now in heaven, 'the days of his flesh:' by *flesh*, meaning not the substance of the human nature, for he retains that still, but the frail quality of subjection to mortality, or possibility.[1] So *flesh* is usually taken, as when all flesh is said to be grass; it is spoken of man's nature, in respect to its being subject to a fading, wearing, and decay, by outward casualties, or inward passions. So in this epistle (2:14), 'Forasmuch as the children', we his brethren, 'did partake of flesh and blood', that is, the frailties of man's nature, 'he himself also took part of the same'. And accordingly the apostle instanceth in the following words of that 14th verse, as in death, which in the days of his flesh

[1] Qu. 'passibility'?—Ed.

Christ was subject to, so also in such frail passions and affections as did work a suffering in him, and a wearing and wasting of his spirits; such as passionate sorrow, joined with strong cries and tears, both which he mentioneth, and also fear, in these words, 'He was heard in that which he feared.' Now these days of his flesh being over and past, for this was only, as says the apostle, in the days of his flesh, hence therefore all such concomitant passionate overflowing of sorrow, fear, *etc.*, are ceased therewith, and he is now no way capable of them, or subjected to them. Yet;—

2. *Positively*. Why may it not be affirmed that for substance the same kind of affection of pity and compassion, that wrought in his whole man, both body and soul, when he was here, works still in him now he is in heaven? if this position be allayed with those due cautions and considerations which presently I shall annex. For, if for substance the same flesh and blood and animal spirits remain and have their use, for though Christ mentioned only his having flesh and bones after his resurrection, unto Thomas and the other disciples, because these two alone were to be the object of his touch and feeling (*Luke* 24:29); yet blood and spirits are included in that flesh, for it is *caro vitalis*, living flesh, and therefore hath blood and spirits that flow and move in it; then why not the

same affections also? And those not stirring only and merely in the soul, but working in the body also, unto which that soul is joined, and so remaining really human affections. The use of blood and spirits is, as to nourish (which end is now ceased) so to affect the heart and bowels by their motion to and fro, when the soul is affected. And why this use of them should not remain (and if not this, we can conceive no other) I know not. Neither why this affection should be only restrained to his spirit or soul, and his corporeal powers not be supposed to communicate and partake in them. That so as he is a true man, and the same man that he was, both in body as well as in soul, for else it had not been a true resurrection, so he hath still the very same true human affections in them both; and such as whereof the body is the seat and instrument, as well as the soul. And seeing this whole man, both body and soul, was tempted, and that (as the text says) he is touched with a feeling in that nature which is tempted, it must therefore be in the whole man, both body and soul. Therefore, whenas we read of the 'wrath of the Lamb' (*Rev.* 6:16), namely, against his enemies, as here of his pity and compassion towards his friends and members, why should this be attributed only to his deity, which is not capable of wrath, or to his soul and spirit only?

And why may it not be thought he is truly angry as a man, in his whole man, and so with such a wrath as his body is affected with, as well as that he is wrathful in his soul only, seeing he hath taken up our whole nature, on purpose to subserve his divine nature in all the executions of it?

But now, how far, in our apprehensions of this, we are to cut off the weakness and frailty of such affections as in the days of his flesh was in them, and how exactly to difference those which Christ had here, and those which he hath in heaven, therein lies the difficulty; and I can speak but little unto it.

Yet, *first*, this we may lay down as an undoubted maxim, that so far, or in what sense his body itself is made spiritual (as it is called, *1 Cor.* 15:44), so far, and in that sense, all such affections as thus working in his body are made spiritual, and that in an opposition to that fleshly and frail way of their working here. But then, as his body is made spiritual, not spirit (spiritual in respect of power, and likeness to a spirit, not in respect of substance or nature), so these affections of pity and compassion do work not only in his spirit or soul, but in his body too, as their seat and instrument, though in a more spiritual way of working, and more like to that of spirits, than those in a fleshly frail body are. They are not wholly spiritual in this sense, that the soul is the sole subject of them, and that it draws up all such workings into itself, so that that should be the difference between his affections now and in the days of his flesh. Men are not to conceive as if his body were turned into such a substance as the sun is of, for the soul, as through a case of glass, to shine gloriously in only; but further it is united to the soul, to be acted by it, though immediately, for the soul to produce operations in it. And it is called spiritual, not that it remains not a body, but because it remains not such a body, but is so framed to the soul that both itself and all the operations of all the powers in it are immediately and entirely at the arbitrary *imperium*[1] and dominion of the soul; and that as the soul is pleased to use it, and to sway it and move it, even as immediately and as nimbly, and without any clog or impediment, as an angel moves itself, or as the soul acteth itself. So that this may perhaps be one difference, that these affections, so far as in the body of Christ, do not affect his soul, as here they did, though as then under the command of grace and, reason, to keep their motions from being inordinate or sinful; but further, the soul being now too strong for them, doth at its own arbitrement[2]

[1] That is, 'power'. —P.
[2] Judgment. —P.

raise them, and as entirely and immediately stir them as it doth itself.

Hence, *secondly*, these affections of pity and sympathy so stirred up by himself, though they move his bowels and affect his bodily heart as they did here, yet they do not afflict and perturb him in the least, nor become a burden and a load unto his Spirit, so as to make him sorrowful or heavy, as in this life here his pity unto Lazarus made him, and as his distresses at last, that made him sorrowful unto death. So that as in their rise, so in their effect, they utterly differ from what they were here below. And the reason of this is, because his body, and the blood and spirits thereof, the instruments of affecting him, are now altogether impassible, namely, in this sense, that they are not capable of the least alteration tending to any hurt whatever. And so, his body is not subject to any grief, nor his spirits to any waste, decay, or expense. They may and do subserve the soul in its affections, as they did whilst he was here; but this merely by a local motion, moving to and fro in the veins and arteries, to affect the heart and bowels, without the least diminution or impair to themselves, or detriment to him. And thus it comes to pass, that though this blood and spirits do stir up the same affections in his heart and bowels which here they did, yet not, as then, with the least perturbation in himself, or inconvenience unto himself. But as in this life he was troubled and grieved 'without sin' or inordinacy; so now when he is in heaven he pities and compassionates without the least mixture or tang of disquietment and perturbation, which yet necessarily accompanied his affections whilst he was here, because of the frailty in which his body and spirits were framed. His perfection destroys not his affections, but only corrects and amends the imperfection of them. *Passiones perfectivas*[1] to be now in him, the best of schoolmen do acknowledge.

Thirdly, All natural affections that have not in them *indecentiam status*, something unbefitting that state and condition of glory wherein Christ now is, both schoolmen and other divines do acknowledge to be in him, *humanæ affectiones quæ naturales sunt, neque cum probro vel peccato conjunctæ, sed omni ex parte rationi subduntur; denique ab iis conditionibus liberantur quæ vel animo, vel corpori aliquo modo officiunt, beatis nequaquam repugnare censendæ sunt.*

> Those affections which are natural to man, and have no adhesion of sin or shame unto them, but are wholly governed by reason, and lastly are exempt

[1] Latin: a perfection of the passions or affections. —P.

from such effects as may any way hurt either the
soul or the body, there is no ground to think that
such affections may not well stand with the state of
souls in bliss,

says Justinian upon this place. Now if we consider
it, Christ his very state in glory is such, as it becomes
him to have such human affections of pity and compassion in his whole man, so far as to quicken and
provoke him to our help and succour: not such as to
make him a man of sorrows in himself again (that
were uncomely, nay, incompatible to him), but such
as should make him a man of succours unto us, which
is his office. To this end it is to be remembered that
Christ in heaven is to be considered, not personally
only as in himself made happy in his Father, but
withal in his relations and in his offices as an head
unto us; and in that relation now he sits there, as
Ephesians 1:21, 22 (and the head is the seat of all the
senses for the good of the body), and therefore most
sensible of any other part. Wherefore because his
members, unto whom he bears this relation, are still
under sin and misery, therefore it is no way uncomely
for him in that estate to have affections suitable to
this his relation. If his state of glory had been wholly
ordained for his own personal happiness, then indeed
there had been no use of such affections to remain

in him; but his relation to us being one, part and ingredient of his glory, therefore they are most proper for him, yea, it were uncomely if he had them not. Neither are they a weakness in him, as so considered, but rather part of his strength, as the apostle calls them, δυναμις. And although such affections might in one respect be thought an imperfection, yet in another respect, namely, his relation to us and office for us, they are his perfection. As he is our head, which he is as he is a man, it is his glory to be truly and really, even as a man, sensible of all our miseries, yea, it were his imperfection if he were not.

And, *fourthly*, let me add this for our comfort, that though all such affections as are any way a burden to his spirit, or noxious to his body, be not now compatible to him; and though that passionate frailty and infirmity which did help him here to pity and relieve men in misery, out of a suffering hurtful to himself; though these be cut off, yet in those workings of affections and compassion which he hath now, which for substance are the same, there is, instead of that passionate frailty, a greater capaciousness, vastness, and also quickness in his affections now in heaven, so to make up a compensation, and so no less effectually to stir and quicken him to relieve us, than those former affections did. For it is certain that as his knowledge was enlarged upon his entering into glory, so his human affections of love and pity are enlarged in solidity, strength, and reality, as true conjugal love useth to be, though more passionate haply at first. They are not less now, but are only made more spiritual. And as Solomon's heart was as large in bounty and royalty as in knowledge, so Christ's affections of love are as large as his knowledge or his power. They are all of a like extent and measure. So far as God's intention to shew mercy doth reach, (and who knows the end of those riches?), so far doth Christ's disposition to bestow it. 'The love of Christ', God-man, 'passeth knowledge' (*Eph.* 3:19). It hath not lost or been diminished by his going to heaven. Though God in his nature be more merciful than Christ's human nature, yet the act and exercise of Christ's affections is as large as God's purposes and decrees of mercy are. And all those large affections and mercies are become human mercies, the mercies of a man unto men.

3. *Privatively.* If these affections of Christ's heart be not suffering and afflicting affections, yet we may, by way of privation, express this of them, that there is a less fulness of joy and comfort in Christ's heart, whilst he sees us in misery and under infirmities,

comparatively to what will be when we are presented to him free of them all.

To clear this I must recall, and I shall but recall, that distinction I made (in the fourth demonstration, sect. 2, part II) of a double capacity of glory, or a double fulness of joy which Christ is ordained to have: the one natural, and so due unto his person as in himself alone considered; the other additional, and arising from the completed happiness and glory of his whole church, wherewith mystically he is one. So in Ephesians 1:23, although he by reason of his personal fulness is there said to 'fill all in all', yet as he is an head in relation to his church as his body, as in the verses before he is spoken of, thus the perfection of this his body's beatitude, it is reciprocally called his fulness; and therefore, until he hath filled them with all happiness, and delivered them from all misery, himself remains under some kind of imperfection, and answerably his affections also, which are suited to this his relation, have some want of imperfection in them, whilst they lie under misery, in comparison of what his heart shall have when they receive this fulness. We may warrantably say Christ shall be more glad then, and is now, as his children are grown up from under their infirmities, and as they do become more obedient and comfortable in their spirits (so *John* 15:10-11). I shall add some illustration to this by this similitude (which though it hold not in all things, yet it will hold forth some shadow of it). The spirits of just men departed are said to be perfect (*Heb.* 12:23), yet because they have bodies unto which they have a relation, and unto which they are ordained to be united, they in this respect may be said to be imperfect, till these bodies be reunited and glorified with them, which will add a further fulness to them. Thus in some analogy it stands between Christ personal and Christ mystically considered. Although Christ in his own person be complete in happiness, yet in relation to his members he is imperfect, and so accordingly hath affections suited unto this his relation, which is no derogation from him at all. The Scripture therefore attributes some affections to him which have an imperfection joined with them, and those to be in him until the day of judgment. Thus expectation and desire, which are but imperfect affections in comparison to that joy which is in the full fruition of what was expected or desired, are attributed to him, as he is man, until the day of judgment. Thus (*Heb.* 10:12-13) he is said to sit in heaven, 'expecting till his enemies be made his footstool;' the destruction of which enemies will add to the manifestative glory of his kingdom. Now, as that will add to the fulness of his greatness, so the complete salvation of his members will add to the completeness of his glory. And as the expectation of his enemies' ruin may be said to be an imperfect affection, in comparison of the triumph that one day he shall have over them, so his joy which he now hath in his spouse is but imperfect, in comparison of that which shall fill his heart at the great day of marriage. And accordingly, the Scripture calls the accomplishment of these his desires a satisfaction; so (*Isa.* 53:11) 'He shall see of the travail of his soul, and be satisfied', which argues desires to be in him, lying under a want of something in the end to be obtained. Only we must take in this withal, that Jesus Christ indeed knows and sees the very time when this his fulness, through the exaltation of his members up to himself, shall be completed, and when he shall trample upon the necks of all his and their enemies; he sees their day a-coming, as the Psalmist hath it, which alleviates and detracts something from this imperfection, that he should thus expect or tarry.

This scruple satisfied, how his heart can be feelingly touched with our sins (our greatest infirmities), seeing he was tempted without sin.

III. There remains one great unsatisfaction to be

removed, which cannot but of itself arise in every good heart. You told us, may they say, that by *infirmities* sins were meant, and that the apostle's scope was to encourage us against them also; and they are indeed the greatest discomforts and discouragements of all other. Now, against them this which the apostle here speaks affordeth us but little, seeing Christ knows not how experimentally to pity us therein, for 'he knew no sin'. Yea, the apostle himself doth here except it, 'He was tempted in all things, yet without sin.' It may comfort us, indeed, that Christ doth and will pity us in all other infirmities, because he himself was subject to the like, but he never knew what it was to be under sin and vexed with lust, as I am; and how shall I relieve myself against that by what the apostle here speaks of him? I shall endeavour to give some satisfaction and relief in this by these following considerations.

First, The apostle puts it, indeed, that 'he was tempted, yet without sin'. And it was well for us that he was thus without sin, for he had not been a fit priest to have saved us else (so *Heb.* 7:26), 'Such an High Priest became us as was separate from sinners, innocent', *etc.* Yet for your relief withal, consider that he came as near in that point as might be. 'He was tempted in all things', so says the text, though 'without sin' on his part; yet tempted to all sin so far as to be afflicted in those temptations, and to see the misery of those that are tempted, and to know how to pity them in all such temptations. Even as in taking our nature in his birth he came as near as could be, without being tainted with original sin, as, namely, by taking the very same matter to have his body made of that all ours are made of, *etc.*, so in the point of actual sin, also, he suffered himself to be tempted as far as might be, so as to keep himself pure. He suffered all experiments to be tried upon him by Satan, even as a man who hath taken a strong antidote suffers conclusions to be tried on him by a mountebank. And, indeed, because he was thus tempted by Satan unto sin, therefore it is on purpose added, 'yet without sin;' and it is as if he had said sin never stained him, though he was outwardly tempted to it. He was tempted to all sorts of sins by Satan, for those three temptations in the wilderness were the heads of all sorts of temptations, as interpreters upon the Gospels do show.

Then, *secondly*, to fit him to pity us in case of sin, he was vexed with the filth and power of sin in others whom he conversed with, more than any of us with sin in ourselves. His 'righteous soul was vexed' with it, as Lot's righteous soul is said to have been with the impure conversation of the Sodomites. He 'endured the contradiction of sinners against himself' (*Heb.* 12:3). 'The reproaches of them that reproached thee', that is, upon his God, 'fell upon me' (*Rom.* 15:3). It was spoken by the Psalmist of Christ, and so is quoted of him by the apostle; that is, every sin went to his heart. So as in this there is but this difference betwixt him and us, that the regenerate part in us is vexed with sin in ourselves, and that as our own sin, but his heart with sin in others only, yet so as his vexation was the greater by how much his soul was more righteous than ours, which makes it up; yea, in that he sustained the persons of the elect, the sins which he saw them commit troubled him as if they had been his own. The word here translated *tempted* is read by some τεπειραμενον, that is, *vexed*.

Yea, and *thirdly*; to help this also, it may be said of Christ whilst he was here below, that in the same sense or manner wherein he 'bore our sickness' (*Matt.* 8:17), who yet was never personally tainted with any disease, in the same sense or manner he may be said to have borne our sins, namely, thus: Christ, when he came to an elect child of his that was sick, whom he healed, his manner was, first by a sympathy and pity to afflict himself with their sickness, as if it had been his own. Thus at his raising of Lazarus, it is said that he 'groaned in spirit', *etc.*; and so by the merit of taking the disease upon himself, through a fellow-feeling of it, he took it off from them, being for them afflicted, as if he himself had been sick. And this seems to be the best interpretation that I have met with of that difficult place in Matthew 8:16-17, where it is said, 'he healed all that were sick: that it might be fulfilled which was spoken by Isaiah the prophet, saying, Himself took our infirmities, and bare our sickness'. Now, in the like way or manner unto this, of bearing our sicknesses, he might bear our sins too; for he being one with us, and to answer for all our sins, therefore when he saw any of his own to sin, he was affected with it, as if it had been his own. And thus is that about the power of sin made up and satisfied.

And *fourthly*, as for the guilt of sin, and the temptations from it, he knows more of that than any one of us. He tasted the bitterness of that, in the imputation of it, more deeply than we can, and of the cup of his Father's wrath for it, and so is able experimentally to pity a heart wounded with it, and struggling under such temptations. He knows full well the heart of one in his own sense forsaken by God, seeing himself felt it when he cried out, 'My God, my God, why hast thou forsaken me?'

Uses of all.

Use 1. Thus that which hath been said may afford us the strongest consolations and encouragements against our sins of any other consideration whatsoever, and may give us the greatest assurance of their being removed off from us that may be; for,

First, Christ himself suffers (as it were), at least is affected under them, as his enemies, which therefore he will be sure to remove for his own quiet sake. His heart would not be quiet, but that he knows they shall be removed. As God says in the prophet, so may Christ say much more, 'My bowels are troubled for him, I remember him still' (*Jer.* 31:20).

Secondly, There is comfort concerning such infirmities, in that your very sins move him to pity more than to anger. This text is plain for it, for he suffers with us under our infirmities, and by infirmities are meant sins, as well as other miseries, as was proved; whilst therefore you look on them as infirmities, as God here looks upon them, and speaks of them in his own, and as your disease, and complain to Christ of them, and do cry out, 'O miserable man that I am, who shall deliver me?' so long fear not. Christ he takes part with you, and is so far from being provoked against you, as all his anger is turned upon your sin to ruin it; yea, his pity is increased the more towards you, even as the heart of a father is to a child that hath some loathsome disease, or as one is to a member of his body that hath the leprosy, he hates not the member, for it is his flesh, but the disease, and that provokes him to pity the part affected the more. What shall not make for us, when our sins, that are both against Christ and us, shall be turned as motives to him to pity us the more? The object of pity is one in misery whom we love; and the greater the misery is, the more is the pity when the party is beloved. Now of all miseries, sin is the greatest; and whilst yourselves look at it as such, Christ will look upon it as such only also in you. And he, loving your persons, and hating only the sin, his hatred shall all fall, and that only upon the sin, to free you of it by its ruin and destruction, but his affections shall be the more drawn out to you; and this as much when you lie under sin as under any other affliction. Therefore fear not, 'What shall separate us from Christ's love?'

Use 2. Whatever trial, or temptation, or misery we are under, we may comfort ourselves with this, that Christ was once under the same, or some one like unto it, which may comfort us in these three differing respects that follow, by considering

First, That we are thereby but conformed to a example, for he was tempted in all, and this may be no small comfort to us.

Secondly, We may look to that particular instance of Christ's being under the like, as a meriting cause to procure and purchase succour for us under the same now; and so in that respect may yet further comfort ourselves. And,

Thirdly, His having once borne the like, may relieve us in this, that therefore he experimentally knows the misery and distress of such a condition, and so is yet further moved and quickened thereby to help us.

Use 3. As the doctrine delivered is a comfort, so the greatest motive against sin and persuasive unto obedience, to consider that Christ's heart, if it be not afflicted with—and how far it may suffer with us we know not—yet for certain hath less joy in us, as we are more or less sinful, or obedient. You know not by sin what blows you give the heart of Christ. If no more but that his joy is the less in you, it should move you, as it useth to do those that are ingenuous. And take this as one incentive to obedience, that if he retained the same heart and mind for mercy towards you which he had here on earth, then to answer his love, endeavour you to have the same heart towards him on earth which you hope to have in heaven; and as you daily pray, 'Thy will he done on earth as it is in heaven.'

Use 4. In all miseries and distresses you may be sure to know where to have a friend to help and pity you, even in heaven, Christ; one whose nature, office, interest, relation, all, do engage him to your succour; you will find men, even friends, to be oftentimes unto you unreasonable, and their affections in many cases shut up towards you. Well, say to them all, If you will not pity me, choose, I know one that will, one in heaven, whose heart is touched with the feeling of all my infirmities, and I will go and bemoan myself to him. Come boldly (says the text), μετα παρρησιας, even with open mouth, to lay open your complaints, and you shall find grace and mercy to help in time of need. Men love to see themselves pitied by friends, though they cannot help them; Christ can and will do both.

THE BANNER OF TRUTH

The Banner of Truth Trust originated in 1957 in London. The founders believed that much of the best literature of historic Christianity had been allowed to fall into oblivion and that, under God, its recovery could well lead not only to a strengthening of the church today but to true revival.

Inter-denominational in vision, this publishing work is now international, and our lists include a number of contemporary authors along with classics from the past. The translation of these books into many languages is encouraged.

A monthly magazine, *The Banner of Truth*, is also published and further information will be gladly supplied by either of the offices below.

3 Murrayfield Road  PO Box 621, Carlisle
Edinburgh, EH12 6EL   Pennsylvania 17013,
UK   USA
www.banneroftruth.co.uk